# LIVING TH

EXPLORING
FAITH
*Theology for Life*

SERIES EDITORS: Leslie J Francis and Jeff Astley

# LIVING THEOLOGY

**Michael West**

**Graham Noble**

**Andrew Todd**

DARTON·LONGMAN + TODD

First published in 1999 by
Darton, Longman and Todd Ltd
1 Spencer Court
140-142 Wandsworth High Street
London SW18 4JJ

ISBN 0-232-52348-7

A catalogue record for this book is available from the British Library.

Designed by Sandie Boccacci
Phototypeset in Minion by Intype London Ltd
Printed and bound in Great Britain by
Page Bros, Norwich, Norfolk

# CONTENTS

# ACKNOWLEDGEMENTS

We would like to thank all those who have had a hand in the production of this book, wittingly or unwittingly: those with whom we work and reflect about matters theological and educational, and with whom we strive to push back the boundaries of theological education in East Anglia, especially colleagues in the Diocese of St Edmundsbury and Ipswich and on the East Anglian Ministerial Training Course; the students with whom we work on EAMTC and the St Edmundsbury and Ipswich Diocesan Ministry Course, and on the EAMTC MA in Contextual Theology, all of whom have collaborated gladly in the enterprise of theological reflection; those who have assisted us by thoughtfully listening to ideas and reading draft material, especially Catherine Todd; Di Giddons for her assistance with the text; and the editors, Leslie J Francis and Jeff Astley for their help and advice.

# PREFACE

At the beginning of the third millennium a new mood is sweeping through the Christian churches. This mood is reflected in a more radical commitment to discipleship among a laity who wish to be theologically informed and fully equipped for Christian ministry in the secular world.

*Exploring Faith: theology for life* is designed for people who want to take Christian theology seriously. Taken seriously, Christian theology engages the mind, involves the heart, and seeks active expression in the way we live. Those who explore their faith in this way are beginning to shape a theology for life.

*Exploring Faith: theology for life* is rooted in the individual experience of the world and in the ways through which God is made known in the world. Such experience is related to and interpreted in the light of the Christian tradition. Each volume in the series takes a key aspect of theology, and explores this aspect in dialogue with the readers' own experience. Each volume is written by a scholar who has clear authority in the area of theology discussed and who takes seriously the ways in which busy adults learn.

The volumes are suitable for all those who wish to learn more about the Christian faith and ministry, including those who have already taken Christian basic courses (such as *Alpha* and *Emmaus*) and have been inspired to undertake further study, those preparing to take theology as an undergraduate course, and those already engaged on degree programmes. The volumes have been developed for individuals to work on alone or for groups to study together.

Already groups of Christians are using the *Exploring Faith: theology for life* series throughout the United Kingdom, linked by an exciting initiative pioneered jointly by the Anglican dioceses, the Board of Education of the Church and World Division and the Ministry Division of the Archbishops' Council of the Church of England, the National

Society and the Church Colleges. Used in this way each volume can earn credits towards one of the Church Colleges' Certificates and provide access to degree level study. Further information about the Church Colleges' Certificate Programme is provided on page 107.

The Church Colleges' Certificate Programme integrates well with the lifelong learning agenda which now plays such a crucial role in educational priorities. Learning Christians can find their way into degree-bearing programmes through this series *Exploring Faith: theology for life* linked with the Church Colleges' Certificates.

In preparing a series of this kind, much work is done behind the scenes. Financial and staff support have been generously given by the Ministry Division. Thanks are due to Marilyn Parry for the vision of bringing together the Aston materials and the Anglican Church Colleges of Higher Education. Thanks also should go to the Aston staff and the original authors for being willing to make the materials available for reworking. We are also grateful for financial support from the following Church Colleges: Chester College; Christ Church University College, Canterbury; The College of St Mark and St John, Plymouth; St Martin's College, Lancaster; Trinity College Carmarthen; and Whitelands College (Roehampton Institute). Without the industry, patience, perception, commitment and skill of Ruth Ackroyd this series would have remained but a dream.

The series editors wish to express their personal thanks to colleagues who have helped them shape the series identity, especially Diane Drayson, Ros Fane, Evelyn Jackson, Anne Rees and Morag Reeve, and to the individual authors who have produced high-quality text on schedule and so generously accepted firm editorial direction. The editorial work has been supported by the North of England Institute for Christian Education and the Centre for Theology and Education at Trinity College Carmarthen.

Leslie J Francis
Jeff Astley

# INTRODUCTION

This book is not about reading theology, discussing theology, or even doing theology, but about *living* theology. At its heart is an understanding of theology which seeks to bring our present context and experience into a vital and critical dialogue with the riches of the Christian tradition. This is theology which is both personal and communal, touching every part of our individual lives while promoting an engagement with the faith community, past and present. It is a theology that demands that we act on the basis of critical reflection as we learn to explore the contexts in which meaning is constructed.

It is theology that needs to be lived, because it encounters the living, the life-giving, God.

Accordingly, the book balances the need to understand our present situation with the need to enter into our theological inheritance. Following the first chapter, which asks the question 'What is theology?', chapters 2, 3 and 4 look at the present dimension. They focus on: the art of story-telling and its contribution to meaning-making; ways of engaging with our contexts, local and global; the dimension of theology which involves seeing things afresh, new ways of knowing God and ourselves; and the role of 'thick descriptions' which enable us to view things from a number of different perspectives and discern the right response or action.

Chapters 5, 6 and 7 focus more fully on the tradition, exploring ways in which the stories of previous generations of those who encountered God also represent a response to particular contexts, ways of articulating a vision and a knowledge of God, and the attempt to discern the right action to take in particular situations. These chapters, drawing on modern scholarship, look at the ongoing dialogue between present experience and inherited wisdom in the Old Testament, the New Testament and the first few centuries of the Christian church.

The remaining chapters highlight and develop the search for ways of integrating past and present. Chapter 8 considers some of the challenges inherent in living in a post-modern society, and in seeking at the same time to live out a vision of a Kingdom of God which is both now and not yet. Chapter 9 pursues the theological engagement through the story of Tom, a middle manager seeking to live theology in the context of making people redundant. Chapter 10 draws together and articulates the model of living theology which grows and develops throughout the book, and seeks to help the reader identify a way forward.

# 1. LIVING THEOLOGY

## Introduction

This chapter opens with some thoughts about how people begin to do theology. It examines traditional ways of doing theology, especially biblical studies and systematic theology. In addition the chapter looks at challenges to traditional thinking, which come from feminist and liberation theologies. This sets the scene for an exploration of the dialogue which takes place in theology today between our present experience and our faith tradition, and begins to open up a discussion of what we might mean by 'living theology'.

This book will take you on a journey into living theology. It will suggest directions in which you might travel, and provide resources that might be useful along the way. But before setting out on that journey it would be good to ask yourself: What is my starting point? Where do I begin to do theology? How do people begin to do theology?

---

### Reflecting on experience
What does theology mean to me?

What is my starting point for exploring living theology?

Where do I begin to do theology?

What important experiences do I bring with me?

---

## Theologians' tales

For Jo the moment of realisation came as she was walking in the mountains. She was suddenly struck by her own smallness, and by the immensity of creation. And yet she mattered to something, someone beyond the universe, who was intimately involved with it and her.

For David it was as he received communion, something he had done hundreds of times before. But this time was different. He suddenly realised what St Paul meant by saying that communion was a way of 'proclaiming the Lord's death'. It meant that Jesus was still committed to sharing in the world's suffering and that he, David, could no longer ignore it.

For Sally it happened the other way round. As a social worker she was well aware of the injustice of society and the need for action. She came to the vicarage to challenge the vicar into supporting her work. She found a fellow traveller, a priest who was also committed to justice, and stayed to talk political theology.

Janet came seeking to escape the world. She was disillusioned with talk of 'progress', of 'rising standards of living'; she had been let down by such words before. She came to church seeking a better hope, and found it helped her to live in the present.

Michael was kneeling in Julian of Norwich's cell when it happened. He discovered that words no longer mattered, that he had dropped into another dimension: the silence which is beyond words. And yet here he encountered not nothingness, but everything.

Alan was a student doing biblical studies, fascinated by the different critical approaches to the Bible. During his third year he discovered narrative criticism, which approached the text as story, with characters, action, dialogue. For the first time he began to enter into the text, to make contact between its story and his own.

Sheila was a scientist, a physicist. She had recently begun work on probability, and was suddenly struck by the improbability in a vast universe of a planet on which life had come into existence. She was suddenly faced with the only logical answer: that God existed.

The people above (and the real people who lie behind the stories) began to do theology, to live theologically, because of a variety of encounters: with their own experience; with a revelation of God; with scripture; with the Christian tradition; with their own culture; with reason. These are the six 'formative factors in theology' identified by John Macquarrie (1966), in *Principles of Christian Theology*.

**EXERCISE**

Can you make any connections with the stories told above, or can you tell of a different experience?

What was it that you encountered: experience, revelation, scripture, tradition, culture, reason? Or would you use some other word to describe what you met?

How might your experience become a starting point for doing theology?

## What is theology?

To identify a beginning is not, of course, to describe what theology is. Further thought is needed to be in a position to say what happens next; to say how one might proceed from the point of beginning; to indicate what is involved in continuing to be a theologian. This is the area on which we focus next, as we seek to answer the central question: what is theology?

**EXERCISE**

Before reading about the different approaches to theology which follow, ask yourself again the key question: what is theology? Jot down key words which describe what theology is about (for example, God, Bible, books, life, study, church, universities, work, play, etc.).

For some people theology is the preserve of academic theologians, people who study theology from books and then go on to write more books! That is not the assumption behind this book, which is that *you* are a theologian, whatever your context. Nonetheless, doing theology together will involve some understanding of theology as it is undertaken in universities, its contribution to a wider theological picture, and its challenges. Insights from academic study will inform every chapter, although perhaps especially chapters 5, 6 and 7. At this

point, however, we will begin to get our bearings by looking at two
of the major academic disciplines: biblical studies and systematic
theology.

## Biblical studies

The major source for biblical studies is the Bible, although reason is also
formative. (Biblical studies, as with any academic discipline, could not
proceed without reasoned argument.) The major approach for the last
two centuries in biblical studies has been historical. This has involved
setting the Bible in its historical context, looking at the history of the
text, and at the history behind the text. More recently biblical studies
has also adopted a variety of literary approaches to the text, seeing it as
story, for example. Whichever approach is taken the biblical text is the
focus and is regarded as primary. Books about the text (such as
commentaries) are regarded as being secondary. Within the field of
biblical studies, Old and New Testament studies represent the major
sub-divisions of the subject, while different ways of approaching the
text attract particular groups of scholars.

The theology of biblical studies is rooted in an understanding of the
Bible as the revelation of God. Within the historical approach, this can
mean seeing revelation as something which took place in the past, when
the texts were written. In consequence, the term 'biblical theology' is
often used to mean the theology done by historical figures (people in
ancient Israel, the Jews, the first Christians). Later theology is then seen
as a reflection on biblical theology, a response to God's revelation in the
Bible. A number of tendencies exist within this area of theology. On the
one hand, there is a tendency to search for *the* meaning of the text. On
the other hand, biblical studies can become a study of the history of
religions, with little involvement on the part of the scholar. At its best,
however, biblical studies plays a key role in illuminating the text.

## Systematic theology

Systematic theology also draws on the Bible and reason as major
sources. However, in this discipline the 'tradition', the writings of
theologians who came after the time of the Bible, is also a key source.
The aim of the subject is to arrive at systematic expressions of the
Christian faith, or to examine those expressions. The aim may be to
describe, indicating the shape of Christian belief, or to prescribe, setting
forth what Christianity demands of the believer. Sub-divisions are:
theology (about God); christology (about Christ); soteriology (about

salvation); ecclesiology (about the church) and eschatology (about the end, judgement and what lies beyond). In approaching these subjects systematic theologians may work historically (giving an historical outline of belief), or philosophically (looking at the logic of belief); or they may combine the two approaches.

Systematic theology makes the assumption that God is knowable (while also acknowledging that God is unknowable). The Bible is a source for understanding the revelation of God, but God is revealed in other ways too, not least in history. If biblical studies is textual, then systematic theology is conceptual: it is interested in ideas. (Neither subject is primarily practical, although both may be 'applied', often by people other than those who study them.) The tendency of systematic theology is towards dealing with abstract ideas. It may also seek sometimes to harmonise conflicting ideas, rather than living with contradiction. Yet the great strength of systematic theology is that it encourages people to ask: what do we believe?

The two subjects play a major part in the theological scene. They have fed the churches in their preaching, in their reflection, and in their pastoral care. They continue to inspire people to worship God. However, in recent years theologians have been powerfully reminded that biblical studies and systematics do not represent a total definition of theology. New perspectives have been brought to bear, which challenge those who pursue the traditional disciplines to recognise that there are other dimensions to theology than dealing with texts and ideas. Further, such challenges have asked those who pursue biblical studies and systematic theology to examine their assumptions and values.

## Feminist theology

Thus, for instance, a recent challenge to biblical studies comes from feminist theologians. They point out that every stage of the history of the Bible (its composition, transmission, translation, interpretation) has been shaped by men. The Bible has been used to oppress women, to keep them 'in their place'. Biblical studies has been overwhelmingly androcentric, in other words, growing out of the experience of men. Yet this has been presented as the 'common-sense' approach to the Bible. The Bible has not been (as the revelation of a just God should be) an instrument of liberation for women (see Fiorenza, 1983, part 1).

Feminist biblical criticism has a number of implications for biblical studies. Discovering the 'meaning' of a text is not enough if it does not lead to liberation. No interpretation of the Bible is 'neutral'. The dialogue between the Bible and experience (especially that of women) is an essential part of interpreting and appropriating the text. Revelation is not presented on a plate as a gift from the past; it needs to be discovered and tested in the present.

## Liberation theology

Similarly, liberation theology (for instance, from Latin America) poses a challenge to systematic theology. From this context comes the criticism that the Christian faith has been used to justify the oppression of the poor and needy (not least through its support for, and involvement in, both imperialism and colonialism). The criticism is that systematic theology is the preserve of the experts and church authorities. It is intrinsically hierarchical. Christian theology has grown out of a (largely) European context, without recognising how culturally dependent and ideological it is. Systematic theology has excluded the marginalised, where it should (according to its own principles) have empowered and liberated them (see Rowland, 1988, chapter 5).

The implications for systematic theology are many. Concepts are no good without action ('orthodoxy' needs to be matched by 'orthopraxy', that is, right action). Systematic theology needs to be done by the whole church. There needs to be a real dialogue between theology and culture. The Christian faith should be involved in redemption rather than just talking about it!

Feminism and liberation theology suggest new ways of doing theology. These ways involve paying attention to people's experience as a primary 'text', being suspicious about the assumptions which underlie people's theologies, and being aware of the cultural setting of theology. Such theology assumes that God is revealed not only in the texts and ideas of the past, but in people's lives today. There is a concern that theology should involve right action, as well as discovering the right words, and should be open to all, rather than the preserve of experts. Such an approach does not involve the rejection of biblical studies or systematic theology. Rather it suggests that such academic disciplines must be subject to the critical appraisal of those who find theology done to them, rather than by them. This sort of critical dialogue between study and life is one of the major aims of this book. Indeed, the new approach to theology outlined above forms a major context for the 'living theology' found in these pages.

## Moving on

Looking at different ways of doing theology, discovering where we began to do theology (or resolving to begin now), exploring what theology is, raises the question of how we go forward from here. How can we explore further why we are interested in theology? How is it possible to pursue different strands of theology? How can we live theology?

This book will suggest a particular way forward. It will seek to establish a number of the dimensions of living theology. The starting point will be story-telling, a basic tool in the theologian's tool box. Stories are a way of articulating meaning, indeed of making meaning. Through stories (our own and those of others), our experience, our encounters, our understanding of who and where we are, and our vision of God come to have a shape. Stories enable us to grapple with meaning and enter into dialogue with it. They allow it to touch us at the heart of our being. There will be the opportunity in chapter 2, therefore, to open up a number of windows onto story: to explore the story-teller's art; to engage with the stories which belong to the Christian tradition; to tell your own story. In chapters 5, 6 and 7, there will be an opportunity to look at something of the history of story-telling within the Old and New Testaments and in the life of the early church. This will help us to discover how we are shaped by a tradition of telling and re-telling stories of faith and encounter with God, and to establish further points of contact between our stories and those of our previous generations.

The hope is that you will go on to tell, read and explore stories in order to engage with context, at a local and global level. To grapple with context is to begin to understand how we are shaped not only by our genes but also by our environment. It is also an essential part of seeing how far it is possible, not just to be shaped by our society but to shape it, to change it. Part of exploring context, in chapter 3 and beyond, will be to look at pastoral and prophetic engagement, in the history of Christianity and by living theologians today.

Woven into the fabric of this way of doing theology will also be opportunities to stand back and reflect: to look particularly at what new ways of seeing emerge from telling stories and engaging with context. To see afresh is often to see God in a situation. This, in turn, is to know God in new ways, to grow in relationship with God and God's world. To see from a different angle may be to discover the Kingdom of God and the action, or response, that this requires of us. Once again, it will be possible to look at our own way of seeing, to discover whether our vision can become more multi-dimensional, as well as engaging with ways of seeing revealed by the tradition.

Chapters 2, 3 and 4 will provide the primary opportunities, then, to consider story-telling, how we engage with context, and new ways of seeing and knowing. The constant dialogue between us and previous generations of those who have believed in God will be an integral part of these early chapters. However, chapters 5, 6 and 7 will focus particularly on that dialogue, using story, context and seeing as windows onto our faith tradition. chapters 8 and 9 will look further at the integration of our perspective and that of the tradition. This will involve grappling with the difficulties, challenges and possibilities of attempting such integration in our contemporary context. But the aim will be to discover ways of being living theologians, who respond and act in faith, within the stream of the living history of Christianity. Finally, chapter 10 will provide the opportunity to reassess the ways of doing theology to be found in the book, and to consider further steps on the pilgrimage of living theology.

---

**EXERCISE**

What are your hopes and fears as you set out on the enterprise of living theology?

What areas of your experience do you want to explore theologically?

What ideas would you like to explore?

How would you like to be further equipped as a theologian?

What areas of theology discussed in this chapter attract you as possible subjects to pursue further?

---

## Further reading

Freire, P (1972), *Pedagogy of the Oppressed*, Harmondsworth, Penguin.
Henelly, A T (1995), *Liberation Theologies: the global pursuit of justice*, Mystic, Connecticut, Twenty-Third Publications.

Hogan, L (1995), *From Women's Experience to Feminist Theology*, Sheffield, Sheffield Academic Press.

Morgan, R and Barton, J (1988), *Biblical Interpretation*, Oxford, Oxford University Press.

McGrath, A (1997), *Christian Theology: an introduction* (second edition), Oxford, Blackwell.

Parratt, J (1996), *A Guide to Doing Theology*, London, SPCK.

# 2. TELLING EXPERIENCE

## Introduction

This chapter provides the opportunity to think about the way that we make sense of the world by telling stories. Looking first at the story-teller's art, the chapter continues with examples of stories from our faith tradition with which you can engage as story. In the second half of the chapter, the stories we tell about ourselves become the subject. This will give you the chance to tell your own story and to explore through it the roots of who you are as a person: the origins of your values, beliefs, attitudes and agendas.

---

### *Reflecting on experience*

What stories were important to you as a child?

What stories were important as you grew older?

In what way did you discover the stories: from people, from books, from television or radio?

What meaning did these stories have for you then?

What significance do they have now?

---

## The story

Stories are a very important way in which human beings are able to share their experience and make sense of their lives. They are key ways in which the vast babble of human experience is given coherence and meaning. Stories reflect and shape how we live and are a way of giving meaning to what we perceive, what we do and what we are. To a large extent we learn about our culture through stories, and stories provide the context for our hopes and dreams, our doubts and our faith.

All stories come from a particular culture, a particular context and a particular time and therefore reflect the conventions of their unique situations. However, stories have an appeal and a place in human life that is universal and timeless. A 'good story' will touch the hearts and minds of people across many cultures and epochs of human history.

All story-tellers and all authors of narratives engage in the conventions of their art. The requirements of different genres will give particular shape and linguistic style to their creations. Poetry, history, biography, letter, law, novel and song will all require different strategies and styles at different times and in different cultures, but all will be generative of meaning and insight into the human condition.

All narrators choose their material carefully, select a strategy for telling their stories and emphasise key moments or ideas. Story-telling in its most familiar form requires the narrator to provide for a beginning, a middle and an end to the work, to deal in cause and effect and to engage with motivation and desires. Plot, character, dialogue, context and action add colour and texture to the story-teller's art and encourage engagement with the reader. All stories eventually engage the *story-teller*, the created *text* and the *reader* in a triangular relationship.

The *story-teller* has worked his craft in a particular context, at a particular time, using a particular vehicle or genre. He has had a particular audience in mind and has undertaken the work for a particular purpose. The *text* has been created and is then preserved for the reader. In the fourth book of Rabelais's *Gargantua and Pantagruel*, Pantagruel is far out at sea and is astonished to hear words while seeing no speaker. It transpires that the words had been frozen the previous winter and had thawed with the coming of fair weather. Texts are frozen until warmed by the interest of the reader (Knapp, 1990, chapter 1). The *reader* comes to most texts without a personal knowledge of the author or of his situation and concerns. She does, however, bring a whole set of pre-understandings to the business of reading. These include the beliefs, values, agendas and biases that come from her own life experience, her gender, her ethnic origin and the community in which she grew up. They also include her reason for engaging with the text.

The act of reading a story will therefore consciously or

unconsciously engage the reader in an act of interpretation that will provide a series of interactions involving:
- the genre of the narrative;
- the context in which it was produced;
- the literary strategy of the author;
- the author's intentions and motives;
- the group originally addressed;
- the reader's beliefs, values and agendas;
- the culture from which the reader comes and in which her own life story is set.

Often the reader will need to address these issues if she is to get the most out of the experience.

## Stories of faith

The Christian faith is told in a variety of stories which together weave into a grand narrative of salvation. Each small story is woven into the greater whole to form a faith tradition that comes down to us as scripture, liturgy, creed and practice. The earliest stories from the Jewish scriptures go far back into human history while the newest stories that we weave together in the life of our modern-day churches speak to us of the ongoing journey of faith to which the church is committed.

To understand faith as story is to recognise the various ways in which the encounter with God has been experienced and the means by which it has been passed to the next generation of believers. To tell or write stories is to give coherence and meaning to the experience of God; to read stories is to interpret that meaning for ourselves and for this generation. To search the texts of our faith story is to encounter the God who searches and encounters us.

---

EXERCISE

📖 **Read (out loud if possible) the Book of Jonah in the Old Testament.**

Drawing on the information provided below, examine these issues:
- the nature of the story that is told. Who are the characters ▶▶

and how do they relate to each other? How does the author develop his plot and use character, dialogue and action to weave his story?
- the literary form and strategy of the book. What literary forms are employed and what overall strategy does the author use, and for what purpose?
- how the story relates to the broader story of the people of God. How does the way that God is presented in this book engage with the overall story of salvation history?
- how the story might be interpreted for today.

## Jonah

The Book of Jonah is part of the prophetic literature of the Jewish scriptures and has been preserved among the works of other prophets in the 'Book of the Twelve'. Jonah has been identified with the prophet 'Jonah Ben Amittai' in 2 Kings 14:25 who worked during the days of Jereboam II (786–746 BCE) and the book's position in the scriptures connects it with the work of Amos, Hosea and Micah. This reinforces its traditional association with the eighth century BCE. However, scholars have found the book difficult if not impossible to date with accuracy although some of its language and its ideas about God fit well into the period when the people returned from exile in Babylon. Among the prophetic books that make up the 'Book of the Twelve', it is the only work that is primarily a story that is told about a prophet, and Jonah is the only prophet sent to proclaim God's message in a foreign land.

Although there are several literary forms within the book, including confessions of faith, prophetic sayings, a psalm and a royal proclamation, the Book of Jonah is essentially a *story*. It is clearly designed to be read aloud or told to groups of people, and its use of direct discourse to emphasise the different characters in the story, together with the repetition of key words and phrases, support this. However, it was not written merely to entertain and scholars have abandoned the attempt to treat the book as history. James Limburg (1992, p. 24) describes it as 'a fictional story developed around a historical figure for *didactic* purposes'. This didactic or teaching function provides a clue to the way that the book is organised. Like all good stories the book begins with a tension: the Lord sends Jonah to the great yet wicked city of Nineveh to 'cry against it' (1:2). However, instead of doing this he flees to Tarshish. Having established this tension the author then uses fourteen questions in seven scenes to support a literary strategy that works with this tension to its resolution while teaching the reader about God. For the author, God is the only true God who creates, controls and cares for all the peoples of the earth. He is a God who is just, patient and forgiving and rescues those who call upon him in trouble but who also demands thanksgiving, praise and witness from those who experience his gracious deliverance.

---

**EXERCISE**
📖 **Read (out loud if possible) Psalm 78.**

Drawing on the information provided below, examine these issues:
* the nature of the story that is told. How does the author develop his plot and use character and action to weave his story?
* the literary form and strategy of the psalm. What is the literary form of the psalm and why has it been constructed in this way?
* how the story relates to the broader story of the people of God. How does the way that God is presented in this psalm engage with the overall story of salvation history?
* how the psalm and the story that it tells may best be used today.

---

## Psalm 78

The psalms were composed and set to music to form a key part of communal worship in ancient Israel. They are, by and large, intoned poems of prayer and praise which each had a place in the sequence of worship and a special musical accompaniment. Psalm 78 is subtitled a 'maskil of Asaph'. The term 'maskil' is unclear but 'Asaph' denotes a guild of temple singers within which the psalm may have been composed and handed down. Dating the psalm is difficult but the theology of the psalm suggests that it might have been constructed after the exile in Babylon. Composition, as is common in the Psalms, employs a traditional Hebraic poetic form in which thoughts and ideas are presented in a twofold parallel pattern as in Psalm 78:5:

> He established a decree in Jacob,
> and appointed a law in Israel.

Psalm 78 has the character of an address, given at a festal gathering, and consists of a didactic introduction reminiscent of the wisdom tradition, and two parallel recitals of salvation history. It calls upon the people to attend to the grace and judgement of God that is set out in the sacred tradition and uses this *story* to challenge them to put aside their infidelity. The kingdom had split in two after the death of King Solomon and this psalm further sets out to justify why God had rejected the worship of the northern kingdom and chosen Judah in the south as God's dwelling place.

---

**EXERCISE**
📖 **Read (aloud if possible) the Apostles' Creed.**

Drawing on the information provided below, examine these issues:
- the nature of the narrative. What story is being told?
- the literary form. What is the literary form of the creed and how has it affected its construction?
- the context of the authors. What contexts were they working in?
- how the creed and the story that it tells may best be used today.

---

## Apostles' Creed

> I believe in God, the Father Almighty,
> creator of heaven and earth.
> I believe in Jesus Christ, his only Son, our Lord.
> He was conceived by the power of
> the Holy Spirit
> and born of the Virgin Mary.
> He suffered under Pontius Pilate,
> was crucified, died, and was buried.
> He descended to the dead.
> On the third day he rose again.
> He ascended into heaven,
> and is seated at the right hand of the Father.
> He will come again to judge the living and the dead.

I believe in the Holy Spirit,
the holy catholic Church,
the communion of saints,
the forgiveness of sins,
the resurrection of the body,
and the life everlasting. Amen.

The Apostles' Creed is thought to be a descendant of the earlier Old Roman Creed, which dates from the early third century (Young, 1991, p. 2). The setting for this creed was baptism. As we learn from the instructions on worship given by Hippolytus of Rome, the creed acted as the summary of the Christian faith for those being baptised. It was the form in which they professed that faith. The practice in the early third century was to ask the candidates three questions as they were being baptised. These three questions took the form of one paragraph of the creed, in interrogative form:

• Do you believe in God the Father Almighty ...?
• Do you believe in Jesus Christ ...?
• Do you believe in the Holy Spirit ...?

To each paragraph the candidate replied: I believe.

The creed became known as the Apostles' Creed, not because it went back to the apostles but rather because it expressed the apostolic faith. There is no evidence of creeds before the third century, but they each seek to capture the faith handed on by the apostles to successive generations of Christians. Thus candidates for baptism, in assenting to the creed, were taking on the story of the Christian faith which could be traced back to the time of Jesus. Further consideration of creeds as articulations of the Christian story will be found in chapter 7.

## My story

Where you come from will affect the way that you see things. Graham knows that. He was brought up in a mining village in the Welsh valleys. His father was a miner and when he left school he followed in his footsteps. He moved to England shortly after the mines closed and he now works for an engineering firm in the Midlands. However, the values of comradeship and mutual dependence learned down the pit, the importance of family life, the socialism that was imbibed at his father's knee and the music that filled the chapel of his youth still colour the way he lives his life.

For Judith, the experience of life has been very different. Born in Leeds in 1945 she grew up with post-war rationing. She was happy and secure as a child, did well at school and eventually went to work for the Electricity Board. She married Brian and they had a son. There then followed the worst period of her life. Her marriage broke up and she firmly believes that it was her fault. Looking back she thinks that she suffered badly from post-natal depression, a condition that was not recognised in those days, and is convinced that she drove her husband away. She feels that she let her parents down and brought shame on the family. She is aware that divorce is more common these days and is viewed more sympathetically, but she cannot dismiss a deep sense of guilt which colours the way that she sees herself.

When Sandra hears the word 'Father' in church she thinks of the man who crept into bed with her when she was young and the 'little secret' that they still share. Alan thinks of the absent parent who died when he was two years old. Ann feels the word fails to connect with her experience of being a woman. Andrew was brought up as a liberal Catholic and Diane is a strict Baptist. When they talk about their beliefs they are surprised by how little they share of the same faith.

In many ways our life experience affects our understanding of ourselves, God and church. As theologians we need to be aware of the influences that shape our understanding. To be aware of the values that support the way that we view the world, the attitudes that colour our decisions, the beliefs that support the way that we lead our lives, the hurts that disable us, and the personal agendas that energise our actions is to bring to theology a critical self-awareness.

Beliefs, values, attitudes and agendas are often deeply held. They are forged in a lifetime of experience and do not change until a new insight or fresh understanding demands their reconstruction. However, this means that, although some of our beliefs, values, attitudes and agendas are clear to us, many have lain dormant and half concealed since our earliest experience. Therefore, although they influence the way that we live and act, it is not always clear to us exactly what they are and where they have come from.

Graham still has difficulty relating to the way that his twenty-one-year-old daughter Julie lives her life. He feels that the values that have sustained him seem of little importance and relevance to her. However, he has a strong Christian faith that he expresses primarily in the work that he does among the young people and the unemployed on the estate where he lives, trying to give them something of the sense of belonging and personal value that he has known.

Judith attends her local parish church but has still failed to come to terms with her own sense of unworthiness. She hears the absolution but does not feel forgiven. Why does she feel unable to stand renewed and refreshed? Why does God feel so distant?

It is common today for people or groups to construct 'life history' narratives to help them understand their own lives better and to see the way in which the past has helped to form and inform the present (Denzin, 1987). To tell a story of your life is to give meaning to the past and the present by interpreting what has happened to you. It is to see your life and know it in new ways.

To tell a story of your life is to examine the different ways in which that life was formed and the communities, individuals and organisations that have been of particular importance. The community in which you grew up will have helped form you and parents, teachers, clergy, work colleagues, spouse, children and friends will all have had an impact. The changing experience of home, establishments of education, places of work and different churches may be important reference points. The broader historical context (for example, being a 'war baby' or a 'child of the sixties'), will have played its part. Your gender will also be a key consideration.

To write a story of your life is to recognise what enables and disables the present and to identify the source and strength of those deeply held systems of values, beliefs and attitudes which inform the way that we feel and act. To see these things, and to know them of yourself, brings choices. What is revealed about your deeply held values and beliefs may lead to affirmation or change. Some beliefs and values may feel right to you, others may need to undergo reconstruction in the light of reflection. This process gives you permission to do either. To know where you are 'coming from' is to be able to engage more fully and more creatively in the theological process.

---

**EXERCISE**
Describe your present life. How do you spend your time? Would you like to spend your time differently? Who are the ▶▶

significant people at present? Are they different from the past? How would you describe your faith to another person? How often do you go to church and why? In what ways has your understanding of your faith changed in recent years?

Take a piece of paper. Write your name in the centre and put the people you know around your name. Put them closer to you if you enjoy their company. Put those you spend most time with in larger print. Underline family.

Reflect on the exercise. Do the results surprise you, worry you or reassure you?

Keep the chart for a further exercise in chapter 3.

**EXERCISE**

Using a large piece of paper map out your life history. You could, for example, split your life into 'pre-school', 'primary school', 'upper school', 'young adult', ('early married',) 'middle age', 'approaching retirement', 'early retired'.

Under each heading answer the following questions. Where were you living? What are your main memories and feelings of this time? Who were the significant people for you? What were your beliefs? How was faith expressed? What were the key institutions that you belonged to and how did you feel about them? What was going on in the world at the time?

Now consider the following questions. What are the values that you live by and where have they come from? What attitudes colour your view of the world and when and where did you adopt them? What beliefs are important to you and where were they born? What priorities do you give time to and why?

---

**EXERCISE**

In the light of the process of 'seeing and knowing' undertaken above, write a brief 'life history' narrative. You may choose the genre. It could be in the form of a short story, a letter, a CV in support of a job application, a script prepared for 'This is your life' or any other appropriate literary form. Make sure that the way that you write and your use of plot, character and action is appropriate.

---

## Further reading

Aveyard, I (1997), *God Thoughts: a starter course in theological reflection*, Nottingham, St John's Extension Studies.

Ballard, P and Pritchard, J (1996), *Practical Theology in Action*, London, SPCK.

Ford, D (1990), Narrative theology, in R J Coggins and J L Houlden (eds), *A Dictionary of Biblical Interpretation*, pp. 489–491, London, SCM.

Graham, E (1996), *Transforming Practice*, London, Mowbray.

# 3. ENGAGING CONTEXT

## Introduction

This chapter is about contexts and how we are shaped by them. It looks at global and local contexts which provide the settings for stories and their interpretation. An opportunity is provided for thinking about how we can explore our own local situation and community. Finally, the chapter looks at the tension, seen in the Bible, between being a part of culture and seeing the world around us through the eyes of faith. Prophetic and pastoral ways of addressing this tension are addressed through particular biblical texts.

---

### *Reflecting on experience*

Do you know more about your local community or about world situations?

How does information reach you about the local and the global?

Have you experienced conflict between your faith and being a member of society?

---

## Local and global contexts

From the moment that we are born we become children of our time. Our DNA has gifted us with a unique combination of genes that will provide both physical and emotional traits. These will affect our health and personality and may even have a bearing on the length of our lives. However, the culture into which we are born is going to provide us with the basic set of contexts in which our lives will be formed and the 'tool box' of language and social behaviour with which we can construct our unique selves (Bruner, 1990, chapter 1). As we noted in the previous chapter, experience of such institutions and groups such as home, school, work, and church, constructed in the context of late twentieth-century local, national and global culture, will have already helped to make us what we are. Our language, dress, interests and beliefs will be coloured by the hand that nature has dealt us and the choices we have made. Our past will inform our present and help determine our future. But it is to the present contexts in which our lives are lived that we now turn.

The social pattern of our lives at the turn of the millennium is clearly different from that of previous generations. Although a level of change is to be expected as each generation succeeds the previous one, the extent and speed of change during this period of human history is unprecedented. In chapter 8 we will investigate our present-day context in greater detail. For now we need to be aware of the different dimensions that affect the way we lead our lives.

The first set of contexts revolves around the local. The local is in one sense a geographical entity. It is the place in which we live. We may work close by or travel some distance to a workplace. We may work from home. Either way our life has certain geographical boundaries within which we understand what it means to be local. However, these may be at odds with our sense of identity or allegiance. Because we live in a particular geographical area does not necessarily mean that we call that home. Our emotional involvement may well be with a community five miles away, across the other side of Britain or even abroad. This is related to the fact that access to transport and many forms of instant communication have changed the way that we lead our social lives. The people or groups of people with which we choose to spend our time may bear little resemblance to the geographical place in which we live. The car may have stimulated this revolution but the Internet will eventually carry it to new levels. This has led sociologists to talk about social relationships in terms of networks of time: the time that we spend in different sets of relationships with different individuals and groups. Put together, networks of time provide a fascinating insight into the lifestyles and social contexts of individual people.

The second set of contexts is global. The way that the world community interrelates with the local is growing in significance (Giddens, 1990, pp. 63ff). Our televisions beam news from across the world so that most of us know more about what is happening in the White House than in the local town hall. The world economy has linked the fortunes of countries together in unprecedented ways and the political independence of the nation state is being pressured on the one hand by the need for broader alliances across continents and on the other hand by a growing regional identity. The revolution in the world of business and commerce and its effect on the experience of work; the revolution in the roles of men and women and its effect on marriage and sexual relationships; and the revolution in transport and communication and its effect on social relationships, provide a global context which touches our lives at every point. The church has not remained untouched by this radical change. Like an individual, the story that it tells about itself, the values, beliefs, attitudes and agendas that come through its history, have a significant effect on its present life. But also like individuals, the way that the church community leads its life and undertakes its work will be affected by the local and global contexts which affect society at large and its own membership.

Janet is a trainee Reader in the Church of England who had been asked to undertake a project designed to help her and her local church community at St Gregory's reflect on their history and to identify what they valued from the past. They had then to consider what strategies might be needed for the church to minister more effectively to people today. By listening to the stories of individuals, interviewing previous clergy and churchwardens, looking through records, reading two local histories that she found in the library, and familiarising herself with an overview of the history of the Church of England, Janet was able to identify some key values and beliefs that were still deemed to be of importance. It seemed to matter to people that the Church of England was the national church committed to the care of every person in the parish. It was also important that the church shared common worship across the country and even across the world, even though it was getting more difficult to define what that meant.

St Gregory's also had a proud tradition of being evangelical Christians ('but not too extreme, dear') and had always given pride of place to the proclamation of the gospel in the life of the church. Recent history, though, had brought change. When the Revd Jeff Smith retired the parish was joined with three others under a younger minister who lived several miles away in one of the other parishes. It was rumoured that he wore vestments ('so Edith said who used to keep the post office') but he was really rather nice. He had a pretty wife ('though she went out to work, dear, unusual at that time') and two teenage children. He had introduced the new services ('which didn't make him very popular in the beginning') and started a monthly family service which had brought some new people into church. The new vicar has seven churches. He tells everybody that unless St Gregory's develops local ministry, then the church will not be able to carry on; he has even talked about ordained local ministry. They need to get a team of people together to take the services and visit the sick ('not that they'll like it if it isn't the vicar that calls to see them').

Janet, and the group that was working with her, identified several ways in which the church could value its past while moving forward into the future. However, the overriding issue for Janet herself was the need to value people in the work they were already doing and to equip them more effectively to live their theology at home, at work, in the community and at church. The proud evangelical tradition of their church demanded that the gospel was proclaimed at every opportunity and in every situation.

Brian and Bill had urged their parish church to undertake a 'mission audit'. They were concerned that their church did not have enough information about the community in which it was set or about the lives of individuals that it was committed to serve. As usual with church councils, the idea was considered to be a very good one as long as it did not cost anything and as long as Brian and Bill organised it. Bill had collected several documents on the subject from the diocesan resource centre, and had got interested in the idea of 'networks of time'. He thought that he should start with himself and tried to map out his own 'networks' on a piece of paper (figure 1). He found it quite difficult to do and realised when he had finished that there was a lot more detail that could have been added. It also confirmed to him why he had had that 'mild' heart attack two years ago. That was also when he had joined the Franciscans, looking for a quiet, solid centre to his life. School had been partly the problem. He had only just escaped redundancy during the last round of cutbacks, and successive governments' interference with the education system had left him feeling disillusioned and ready to consider early retirement. All in all the picture depressed him. He smiled when he thought of the house group and the worship group in the church. Those he really enjoyed, but he could not remember how he had got involved with deanery synod and diocesan finance, and was not clear how he was expressing his faith in ways that touched the lives of others. Certainly there were areas of his life that seemed to be contained in separate compartments where his faith was rarely, if ever, relevant to what was happening. The gardening had been important to him but he had seemed to lose his enthusiasm in recent years. Strange, that. He would have thought that gardening would become more important as he got older. Perhaps it was time to take a good look at his life and decide what God might want of him in the future.

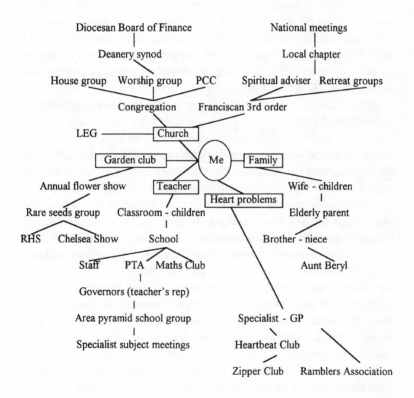

Figure 1: Bill's Personal Network

Brian had been busy with the community while Bill was becoming depressed by his own network chart. He was going to persuade Bill to get others in the community to draw similar network charts. These could then be used to help the church see where members of the local community were spending their time and how much they were investing in the community in which they lived. He had also recruited others for a job that can best be described as community mapping. He had organised a group for Friday evening who were going to 'walk the community'. It would be light until about 9.30p.m. and would give ample time to just walk around and get a feel of the place. His son Adam had decided that he would get up early one morning and follow the postman. He thought that that would be the very best way of understanding where everybody lived and what distances were involved. Brian thought it was an excellent idea but was unsure whether Adam would ever get up that early to undertake it. Mary and her husband Simon had volunteered to spend some time in the library getting what information they could from census data, maps, agency reports, anything really that they could lay their hands on. Simon said that his brother was on the Internet and was downloading a report that the local authority had commissioned on poverty in the county. Brian had decided that he would talk to some of the professionals in the area. He knew the local headmaster and would have no difficulty talking to the doctor because he was currently churchwarden. The policeman might be another useful contributor and he would have to find out whether it would be possible to talk to a social worker. Another idea that had occurred to him when he had been walking the dog was that the community changed at night and at weekends. It might also change at different times of the year. This would need to be investigated. He was pleased that the audit was receiving such good support. People seemed genuinely interested. Indeed several church people had already stopped him to tell him what they thought the community was like. That had given him the idea for the focus group. That would involve getting representatives from different sections of the community to talk about what it was like to live here.

More than once he had stopped to wonder why he was really doing this. Was it just to help the church know the context in which its life and work was set, or was it to challenge the church to respond to what he found? Already he knew that there was genuine poverty in their midst, people without transport unable to get out of the community to visit friends or shop, young single parents without support, elderly people who were desperately lonely. There were people that could be helped by willing volunteers from the church, but if the lives of others were to change, local and national government policy would need to be challenged. He wondered how the church council would respond to that.

---

**EXERCISE**

In chapter 2 you were invited to undertake an exercise in which you placed yourself in the centre of the piece of paper and put the people you know around your name. Using this as a starting point, draw your own personal network chart. Include all the organisations to which you belong.

Reflect on the chart and address the following questions:
- Does it surprise you, worry you or reassure you?
- What are the contexts in which you live your life?
- What part does your faith play in these different contexts?

---

**EXERCISE**

Map out a way in which you might investigate the community in which you live or the community that surrounds the church in which you worship. If possible, gather a group of people together and undertake the work.

What are the contexts in which people are living their lives in the local community and what challenges does that present to the church?

---

## Scripture and context

It is easy to forget that the scriptures are themselves the product of the faith community's reflection on the God who revealed himself to them in and through the different cultural contexts in which they lived. These contexts helped to form the way that the people understood their faith and expressed their knowledge of God, while setting up a tension between the way they lived their lives and the demands that their faith placed upon them. The many books of the Old and New Testaments therefore reflect the contexts that gave them birth while expressing the tension that exists at any time between the revelation of God and the religious, social and political contexts of the day (Court, 1997, chapter 6). The Old Testament prophets were nurtured in the traditions of their day yet railed against kings, priests and people on behalf of the poor and oppressed. They warned against inappropriate foreign alliances and the people's acceptance and worship of other gods. The Gospel writers show Jesus as a Jew of his time yet sharp in his criticism of much of the tradition that had come down to him through scribes and Pharisees. St Paul and St John the Divine both ministered in a first-century world dominated by the Roman empire but both came to a very different view about the way that the church should engage with it. Paul, a Roman citizen, believed it brought stability to the world and would aid the spread of Christianity and was to be supported. Through his prophecies in the Book of Revelation, John challenged the Roman empire as essentially evil and condemned it for being in sharp conflict with gospel values and beliefs.

Indeed, the relationship that the gospel and therefore the scriptures have to any culture at any time has always been a matter of keen debate. The incarnation of Jesus suggests God's intention of making himself known in and through human culture. Because Jesus was a first-century Palestinian Jew and those who wrote the books of the New Testament lived, worked and wrote within this historical, social and political context, the gospel does not come down to us as a pure body of knowledge and teaching, untouched and unsullied by the cultures that gave it birth. It did not drop out of the sky ready formed and able to be translated without difficulty into any other culture or situation. The gospel is 'encultured' and requires careful and critical study before it can confront and converse with the culture of today. That will be true whether the gospel is encountering that culture for the first time or whether there is a 2,000-year history of regular interpretation and rein-terpretation.

Two ways in which the word of God relates to the culture, beliefs and practice of its day, both within the pages of the scriptures and within the life of the church today, is through the ministry of individuals and faith communities that is both *prophetic* and *pastoral.*

Under the heading of prophetic comes those collections of sayings, writings and activities which read the signs of the times, critique society, challenge the faith community itself and present both options and consequences. The great prophets of the Old Testament personify this role but it is one that permeates the New Testament and is a key feature in the life of the church.

Under the heading of the pastoral comes the need for tending, guiding, nurturing and leading which supports and enables faith to grow and develop. This ministry is typified in Israel by the image of the shepherd, and it is with this image that Christ himself and later church leaders are identified. Both prophetic and pastoral ministries combine to build and challenge communities of faith to serve those in need and to oppose the unjust structures of society. Both support and challenge the local and global contexts in which theology is undertaken and ministry is practised.

---

**EXERCISE**

  📖 **Read (aloud if possible) the Book of Amos.** It is a relatively short book and will repay being read at one sitting.

Drawing on the information provided below, examine these issues:
- the geographical, social, religious, political and economic context in which Amos lived and worked;
- the beliefs and values that drove his prophecy;
- how the story of Amos might be interpreted for today.

---

### Amos

Amos came from the small town of Tekoa in Judah, just south of the border with Israel. He prophesied during the time that the kingdom was divided when Uzziah was king of Judah (783–743 BCE) and Jeroboam II was king of Israel (786–746 BCE). Although a southerner by birth he prophesied mainly in Bethel, which was one of the main cult centres in the northern kingdom. By trade Amos was a breeder of livestock and a tender of mulberry trees. During the time that Amos lived, Assyria was the dominant world power but had waned from the time that Shalmaneser III (859–825 BCE) had exacted tribute from Jehu. With the reign of Tiglathpileser III (745–727 BCE), Assyria was looking once more in the direction of Palestine and the northern kingdom was to be overrun by Assyria in 722 BCE. However, in the time that Amos lived there was political calm in the area. This had given rise to a material prosperity which had enabled the rich to get richer and the poor to get poorer. This, according to Amos, had bred social and religious corruption.

The Book of Amos confronts specific situations at a particular period in Israel's history. Amos spoke with the authority of one who stood in the great Mosaic tradition. The people of Israel were God's chosen covenant people but had abused the privilege of their relationship with God. In a covenant relationship the quality of an individual's relationship to God depended on his relationship to his fellow Jews. Social injustice and immorality were therefore entirely unacceptable and would lead inevitably to punishment. Amos addressed his message to the king, the priests and the upper classes, but all Israel would suffer judgement. The worship of Israel flourished in the cultic centres but this smacked of hypocrisy to a prophet who experienced the immorality of these same people in their personal and business lives. Amos worked from the margins of society to challenge the power base at its centre. The people turned a deaf ear to him and even tried to silence him. His prophetic work was to read the signs of the times, critique the society that he encountered, challenge the faith community and show them the consequences of their actions.

---

**EXERCISE**
📖 Read (aloud if possible) 1 Corinthians 11:17–34.

Drawing on the information provided below, examine these issues:
- the geographical, social, religious and political context of the Corinthian church;
- the beliefs and values that drove Paul to write his letter to them;
- how Paul's message to the church at Corinth might be interpreted for today.

---

## Corinth

The situation addressed by Paul when he wrote to the Corinthian church was clearly one of division, which was affecting the celebration of the Lord's Supper. Some of the Corinthians appear to have brought considerable amounts of food and drink to the gathering of the church. Others had nothing to bring. Furthermore, 1 Corinthians 11:33 suggests that some arrived at the gathering sooner, and others rather later. It was in this situation that Paul says that the Corinthians are not eating the Lord's Supper, but their own supper; this is revealed in their inability to wait for latecomers and to share with those who had little. In this situation some were having a party, some were going without.

Gerd Theissen (1982) suggests that there were groups of different social status within the church at Corinth. Such divisions are also reflected elsewhere in 1 Corinthians, for example in attitudes to meat sacrificed to idols revealed in chapter 8 of the letter. So it was the well-off who brought food to the Lord's Supper and were able to arrive early; the poor had little, or nothing to bring, and arrived later, when work permitted. Thus attitudes relating to people's position in the wider society affected their relationship within the church community.

Paul's response to this situation was to take every step to ensure that unity was restored. It was this unity which was at the heart of the Lord's Supper for Paul; that it should be an occasion of division was scandalous. He reminds the Corinthians what is at the heart of the Lord's Supper: the proclamation of Jesus' death 'until he comes'.

## Further reading

Ballard, P and Pritchard, J (1996), *Practical Theology in Action*, London, SPCK.
Green, L (1990), *Let's Do Theology*, London, Mowbray.

# 4. SEEING AND KNOWING

## Introduction

This chapter begins by considering how faith develops when people see things in a new light, or discover new ways of knowing. The second half of the chapter looks at ways in which we can increase our chances of seeing things afresh, by creating 'thick descriptions' of particular situations. These descriptions involve viewing the situation from a number of different perspectives. You will have the opportunity to explore these multi-layered investigations and to see how they may lead to insight and appropriate action.

---

### Reflecting on experience

Can you recall an occasion when 'the penny dropped' and you saw things in a new way?

How does the way you know God now differ from the way you have known God in the past?

Can you think of a situation where you have been helped by seeing things from different viewpoints?

---

## Seeing, believing, knowing

Blind Bartimaeus was sitting by the side of the road when Jesus and his disciples came by. They were in Jericho, which is situated just fifteen miles from Jerusalem. In Mark's Gospel (Mark 10:46–52) the incident is placed at a key point in the narrative. From the moment that Peter had recognised him as the Christ, Jesus' suffering and death had dominated the story. Although the cost of discipleship is laid bare to the reader, the disciples still fail to grasp its implications and to see the truth being unfolded, a situation not uncommon in Mark's Gospel.

Bartimaeus is blind. He sits by the road rather than travelling along it with Jesus. However, as the incident progresses we realise that Bartimaeus is indeed the one who can see because he recognises Jesus as the 'son of David' (the Christ) and calls out to him in faith. Faith has brought spiritual insight and triggers a healing that restores his physical sight. In a story full of irony, Bartimaeus then joins Jesus on the road as a disciple. The road leads to Jerusalem, to suffering and to death, but Mark's story represents a plea to all of us who read his Gospel to have the courage to believe, see and follow.

When Philip says to Nathanael in John's Gospel, 'Come and see' (John 1:46) the invitation to the reader is to see with the eyes of faith and enter into the life that Jesus brings in all its fullness. As the 'light of the world' Jesus promises that 'whoever follows me will never walk in darkness but will have the light of life' (John 8:12). Indeed, sight is a key concept in all of the gospel narratives because it is the appropriate response to the salvation that comes through Jesus Christ. Similarly, blindness is not just a physical incapacity but a symbol for unbelief. Jesus calls the Pharisees 'blind guides of the blind' in Matthew 15:14 and adds that, 'If one blind person guides another, both will fall into a pit', an image that is also found in Paul's letter to the Romans (2:17–19).

The Christian tradition has therefore always lived with the truth that seeing and believing are inextricably linked together in the way that people respond to Jesus and follow him. For many in the gospel seeing leads to believing, while for others believing directs and informs sight. But seeing and believing inevitably lead to knowing. In John's Gospel Jesus, 'the Good Shepherd', says of his sheep, 'I know my own and my own know me' (John 10:14) and he leads those that he knows, calling them by name. But Jesus further teaches his disciples that to know him is to know the Father. 'From now on', he says, 'you do know him and have seen him' (John 14:7).

In John's Gospel Jesus has reminded Thomas and the rest of the disciples that those who have not had the opportunity to see Jesus in the flesh but 'yet have come to believe' are indeed blessed (John 20:29). Not to have seen Jesus in the flesh but to have come to believe in him as the resurrected Lord does however place seeing and knowing into a different context. In his famous 'Hymn to Love' in 1 Corinthians 13, Paul recognises that, in this present age, our ability to see and know God in

Jesus Christ will be curtailed. We can see God now, but not with any clarity. We can know him now, but not in any fullness. However, this will change in the world to come where we will see God 'face to face' and fully know him. This does not mean, however, as Paul recognises, that God cannot fully know us. Indeed, as the great western mystical tradition recognises, our ability to know and love God would not be possible at all without his prior love for us and his revelation of himself in Jesus Christ. In this world God, although not unknowable, is still beyond the power of our comprehension. Discipleship is therefore not possible without the faith, hope and love that characterises the Christian life which in turn must be supported by a willingness to see, know and follow Jesus.

Knowing God in Jesus is therefore never merely an academic pursuit. Thomas à Kempis is perhaps rather scathing of the scholastic tradition when he writes in the first book of the collection *The Imitation of Christ* (1962, p. 37), 'Learned arguments do not make a man holy and righteous, whereas a good life makes him dear to God.' It is true, however, that to know God is to respond to the demands of the Kingdom through loving action. In Jesus' parable in Matthew 25:37–38 the righteous ask the king with some surprise when it was that they saw him hungry, thirsty, a stranger, naked, sick or in prison. They ask because even they, in their goodness, have failed to recognise that they have served the king by serving those in need. Mother Teresa, in the book *Meditations on the Way of the Cross* (1986, p. 8) writes, 'Only by being one with us has he (Jesus) redeemed us. We are asked to do the same; all the desolation of the poor people, not only their material poverty, but also their spiritual destitution, must be redeemed. And we must share it, for only by being one with them can we redeem them by bringing God into their lives and bringing them to God.' To see Christ in the poor and oppressed and to serve him in and through them is a demand for action that stems from knowing and following him.

For Christians today, to see with the eyes of faith, to know and to follow Christ is to attempt to engage with the world, human society and individual people in the light of their creation by God and their redemption through the incarnation, death and resurrection of Jesus Christ. To know Christ is to attempt to see the world through Christ's eyes, even though this may subvert the way that human beings see it. And an important part of this process is to learn to see what is happening in any situation from a variety of different but important perspectives. This will enable the person who wants to 'live theology' to gain a richly textured and varied knowledge of the opportunities that the situation provides for a number of possible gospel outcomes.

---

EXERCISE

📖 Read (aloud if possible) the story of Zacchaeus in Luke 19: 1–10.

Drawing on the information provided below, examine these issues:
- *In the beginning:* What did Zacchaeus see when he encountered Jesus? What did the crowd see? What did Jesus see?
- *In the end:* What did Zacchaeus know about Jesus? What did the crowds know about Jesus? What did Jesus know about Zacchaeus? What did Jesus know about the crowds? What was the outcome?
- How might this story be interpreted for today?

---

## Zacchaeus

The story of Zacchaeus takes place when Jesus is on the road to Jerusalem. At this point in his gospel narrative Luke is using the framework provided by Mark but adds a story of his own. This is either because it came to him already associated with Jericho or because he wanted to use this story, in addition to the healing of the blind man (18:35–43), to emphasise the salvation that came through Jesus in preparation for his arrival in Jerusalem. This incident further contrasts rather neatly with the story of the rich man in 18:18–27. He was a valued son of Abraham who had kept the commandments from his youth yet goes away sad when told to sell all that he has.

Zacchaeus is identified as a 'chief tax-collector' and he clearly had a senior position in the tax system. Also, because Jericho was a wealthy town at that time, it was likely to be an important tax centre. On top of the usual dishonesty that was prevalent among tax-collectors, Zacchaeus would have been considered a Roman collaborator. He would have lost his status as a Jew and would not only have been unpopular but would have been considered an outcast. Jesus' desire to stay at his house would have created a scandal because it would make Jesus guilty by association.

Zacchaeus is generous in his almsgiving because 20 per cent was considered a satisfactory proportion of income to give to the poor.

However, for confessed fraud Roman law demanded a fourfold restitution and this is offered. Salvation restores wholeness to Zacchaeus and his household because through his enthusiastic response and generous promise of restitution he has shown himself a true son of Abraham.

---

EXERCISE
📖 Read (aloud if possible) the story of the prodigal son and his brother in Luke 15:11–32.

Drawing on the information provided below, examine these issues:
- *In the beginning:* What did the prodigal son see when he looked at his inheritance? What did his brother see when he looked at his inheritance? What did the father see?
- *In his need in exile:* What did the prodigal son see and know about himself, his situation and his father? What action did he decide on?
- *When he returned:* What did the prodigal son see? What did his father see? What did his brother see? What did they all know about the situation from their own perspectives?
- How can this story be interpreted for today?

---

## The prodigal son

The parable of the prodigal son and his brother is in a section in Luke's Gospel addressed to the scribes and Pharisees who object to Jesus eating with sinners and keeping their company. It is the third of three parables which Luke then puts together within this common theme. There is joy experienced in heaven over a sinner who repents, and this context is clearly designed to guide our reading.

The parable is a tale told with relish by Luke on a theme that is dear to his heart. The more literary flavour of the piece is emphasised by the use of words and phrases less characteristic of the vocabulary of the Gospels. It is a parable in two parts and scholars have argued about its composition. Was it originally about two sons and was the first part developed at the expense of the second? Was the second part originally intended to be the place where the chief point was to be found; or was the second part merely a later addition to the original parable? Additionally, the relatively modern habit of naming parables will inevitably affect the way that it is understood and interpreted. A parable called the 'prodigal son' will have a different emphasis to one called 'the loving father' and to one entitled 'the two sons'. Indeed this could be seen as a general warning about the practice of giving headings in Bibles.

The parable of the 'loving father' might stress the way that the story describes a God who is loving, forgiving and merciful. This is given liturgical expression in the post-communion prayer in the Church of England ASB Rite 'A' Eucharist (*Alternative Service Book 1980*, p. 144): 'Father of all, we give you thanks and praise, that when we were still far off you met us in your Son and brought us home.' The parable of the 'prodigal son' might stress the pattern of disobedience, repentance and forgiveness experienced by the son who squanders his inheritance, and the parable of the 'two sons' might recognise that the father has two sons who are both ultimately in need of love and forgiveness.

Two further notes may be helpful. It was common practice for a man to make over his property to his heirs during his lifetime by gift of deed while retaining the life rent for himself. Having to feed pigs, considered unclean by Jews, and to do so for a Gentile master, symbolised extreme degradation for a Jew.

## Thick descriptions

A phrase that is increasingly used to describe a situation or incident that can be seen from a variety of viewpoints or perspectives is the term 'thick description'. If a 'thin description' points to one way of seeing and understanding what is happening in any context, then 'thick descriptions' suggest a much more complex and layered understanding of the same situation (Browning, 1991, p. 107).

Typically a thick description can result from the investigation of a situation undertaken from two key perspectives. These could be labelled 'sociological' or 'psychological'. Typically, insights that emerge from a sociological perspective will help a person to see the social dynamics of a situation and the web of relationships that support and inform it. Insights that come from a psychological perspective will help a person to see the effect that individual personality and motivation has on the situation. This investigation will need to place the incident or situation in a set of broader social, political or religious contexts as well as identifying the internal dynamics and personal agendas that help shape it. And of course the eyes through which any person sees when attempting to create a thick description are already significantly affected by their own deeply held beliefs, values, attitudes and agendas, as we saw in chapter 2.

The thick description is therefore a very good vehicle for investigating any situation. Any situation will benefit from being seen from as many perspectives as possible, and time spent in observation will always enrich knowledge. Therefore people who are attempting to live theologically will need to develop ways of 'seeing' that are sensitive to these social and psychological perspectives. One useful way of beginning to weave a thick description is to observe the situation through the eyes of each participant. Ignatian spirituality has long engaged with the scriptures in this way, recognising the need for a personal encounter with the different characters in any situation.

Another useful starting point is to identify what drives and motivates the individuals within the situation. Why are they acting the way that they are and what are they trying to achieve? Although this cannot always be known, situations at work or church often involve people that we have grown to know well, and this knowledge can help inform what is happening. Closely related to this is an investigation into the roles that each person is playing. These roles may be clearly defined or they may be unclear. Questions about role and role conflict may help to identify further perspectives for the thick description.

Another area open to investigation is the contribution that any organisation may make to the way that the situation develops. Organisations have their own working cultures and define the roles of their members in a particular way. A situation in school, hospital or office, or a situation involving professionals from these or other organisations, will be coloured by the culture and working practices that they employ.

Questions that support the development of thick descriptions include:

- questions about the situation: What is the situation? Who was involved? What happened? How did the situation arise? What are the wider set of social, religious or political contexts?
- questions about individuals: What did they do? Why did they act the way that they did? What were their expectations? What roles did they fulfil? What did they want? How were they feeling?
- questions about interaction: What was happening between people? How did the group interact? Who played the dominant role? Was there a victim? Was there a covert process? What was the body language signifying? Was there a common purpose?

- questions about any organisations involved in the situation: What is the organisation involved? Does this situation involve individuals representing any organisation? What way is the organisation and/or an individual representing it affecting the situation?
- questions about me: What did I do? How did I feel? What were my expectations? What role did I fulfil? What was I trying to accomplish? How did my actions affect others? How did my faith affect my actions?

Thick descriptions may or may not be undertaken by people who are themselves involved in the situation under investigation. However, when people are themselves involved, it is important that they are fully aware of the part that they are playing and the influence this is having on others.

Thick descriptions enable individuals to see any situation from a variety of perspectives, which in turn increases their overall knowledge of what is happening at a number of levels. Questions to aid this process might include: What will I learn by reflecting on (i) the behaviour and perspectives of individuals, (ii) the interaction of the group, and (iii) my own practice? How might this inform my ability to see 'with the eyes of faith'?

A final question might then be: How might I best act in this situation in order to promote an outcome consistent with the demands of the gospel?

---

**EXERCISE**

Consider the situation outlined below in the story about John and Michael and address the following questions:

- How might John use the information he already has to create a thick description to help him make up his mind about Michael?
- What more would John need to know?
- How might this help you to see the situation 'with the eyes of faith'?
- What options for action does John have and what do you think he should do?
- Is the thick description enough or does he need more?
- How might the resources of Christian scripture and tradition provide further perspectives?

### John and Michael

John had been asked to visit Michael who is a prisoner in the local young offenders' institution. He is seventeen years old and is serving eighteen months for persistent car theft. He had been a choir boy at St Matthew's until the age of twelve and John's vicar felt that a visit from somebody from the church who was near to his own age would be helpful. John was apprehensive and this feeling had been increased when he talked to a colleague who had visited his brother at the same institution a month previously. He had been searched on entry as part of the recent drive against drug abuse and had met his brother in a very public area within the hearing of a prison officer. The whole experience had been extremely difficult for him and he was not looking forward to his next visit.

Knowing of his likely visit to Michael, John had paid more than usual attention two weeks previously when he had seen his MP on television. John knew that his MP was on the right of the Conservative Party ('to the right of Genghis Khan', his father said) but when he rose at the annual Conservative Party conference to add his views to the debate on 'law and order' John became interested. His speech did not call for the reintroduction of flogging, well not quite. However, he made it clear that those who committed crime (he even mentioned car theft) should be given long sentences in harsh conditions. It needed to be made clear to them that society would not tolerate such behaviour. A clear message that crime does not pay also needed to be sent out to other hooligans who may be similarly tempted.

The social worker who currently sang in the choir did not agree. She did not know all the details of Michael's case but she did tell John after choir practice that she did not feel that a prison sentence would help. The young offenders' institution had a bad record of bullying and drug abuse and, because of overcrowding, there were few opportunities for education. She felt it more likely that prison would further alienate Michael from normal society and make re-offending more likely. This view was largely confirmed by the prison officer who was on the national news that night after another riot in a prison in the Midlands. He was clear that without further government funding and better staff ratios there was little that prison officers could do but lock the prisoners up and keep basic order. As he pointed out with a wry smile, 'I wouldn't want to be locked up with some of the hard cases that we have in here.'

John had also spoken to Michael's mother. He had gone to see her to ask whether she thought that Michael would appreciate a visit, and they got talking about him. She showed him pictures of Michael as a little boy. She was quite open about the fact that she did not know why Michael had got into trouble. If it was her and her husband's fault, she did not know what they had done. They had given Michael a good home and done their best for him. And they were both sticking by him. They visited regularly and they would have him back home when he got out, if he would like to come.

John was struggling to know what to make of Michael. In what light should he see him? Should he visit Michael and, if so, for what purpose?

## Further reading

Ballard, P and Pritchard, J (1996), *Practical Theology in Action*, London, SPCK.

Browning, D (1991), *A Fundamental Practical Theology*, Minneapolis, Minnesota, Fortress.

Green, L (1990), *Let's Do Theology*, London, Mowbray.

# 5. THE LORD'S SONG IN A STRANGE LAND

## Introduction

In chapters 2 to 4, story, engaging with context, and seeing and knowing were explored as different ways of making sense of our encounter with God. In this chapter, these headings become the windows through which we view the different sections of the Old Testament: Torah, Prophets, Writings. In the pages of the Hebrew scriptures, as was indicated above, there are certainly stories: about God, about individuals, about God's people Israel, about Israel's friends and enemies. There is a whole variety of ways of seeing God and God's world; and there are diverse settings or contexts within which stories are told. Once again, an exploration of these leads the reader into an encounter with God, the God of Israel, the God who made heaven and earth.

---

*Reflecting on experience*
How important is the Old Testament to you?

Which Old Testament stories are significant for you?

What is your reaction to the thought of studying the Old Testament?

Do the churches you have known value the Old Testament?

---

## The Old Testament

The Old Testament, or Hebrew scriptures, represents an amazing collection of writings. The history of the events recounted in its pages spans more than 1,000 years. It includes stories of Israel's ancestors, of the Israelites in Egypt, of their exodus from Egypt and journey to the Promised Land, of their growth as a nation, of the division of Israel into two kingdoms and their fall, of the exile in Babylon and of the Jews' return to Jerusalem. It contains an enormous diversity of genres, everything from legend to love poetry, oratory to oracles, proverbs to praise, hymns to history. It has narratives of epic propor- tions (dealing with, for example, creation, or the exodus from Egypt), but it also contains intimate stories of particular individuals (such as that of Ruth, which will be explored in this chapter). All the great themes are here: human nature, the character of God, birth, life and death.

The Jews, with whom the Hebrew scriptures originated and for whom they are still sacred texts, divided the scriptures into three cate- gories: Torah, Prophets, Writings. The following texts are often grouped under these headings:

**Torah**
- Genesis, Exodus, Leviticus, Numbers, Deuteronomy

**Prophets**
- The Former Prophets: Joshua, Judges, 1 and 2 Samuel, 1 and 2 Kings
- The Latter Prophets: Isaiah, Jeremiah, Ezekiel, 12 'minor' prophets

**Writings**
- 1 and 2 Chronicles, Ezra-Nehemiah, Daniel
- The Psalms
- Job, Proverbs
- The Song of Songs, Ruth, Lamentations, Ecclesiastes, Esther

## Torah: the law of the Lord

Torah consists of the first five books of the Bible (the Pentateuch). These are also known by both Jews and Christians as the five books of Moses, although it is clear today that they were not written by Moses. But what is Torah? One translation of this Hebrew word is Law, but this can be misleading. Some of the material in Torah is in the form of legal codes, but there is much more to the Pentateuch than that.

The codes that exist within Torah, governing the behaviour of God's people, are set in a narrative framework. The setting of the legal material is the story of God's people Israel, a complex, epic tale. This has often been described as 'salvation history', an account of God's dealings with the people chosen by God, God's saving acts on their behalf. The story invites the reader to journey through Israel's pre-history, which includes the creation of the heavens and the earth, the flood, the legends of Israel's forebears. It encourages us to identify with the Israelites in slavery in Egypt, and walk with them on their exodus from Egypt, through many adventures until they come to the Promised Land.

At the heart of Torah is the emerging relationship between God and Israel. This relationship is rooted in the idea of the covenant. In one sense this is about a binding agreement between two people, but once again the concept goes beyond the legal. God's covenants with people like Noah, Abraham, his family and descendants, Moses and the Israelites are about a relationship based on mutual faithfulness. Further, encapsulated in covenant is the idea of promise, the promise that God will be with God's people, providing for them (Clines, 1978). Covenant creates two possibilities: blessing for those who keep it, curse for those who do not.

The legal codes of the Pentateuch emerge, then, out of this narrative setting as the parameters of the covenant relationship. The codes also emerge out of Israel's need to understand how they can worship the God who has called them into a relationship and adopted them. They relate, for instance, to the Ark of the Covenant, the symbolic focus for worship, or to sacrifice, indicating appropriate offerings to God. These cultic regulations are, however, no less entwined with Israel's story. The Ark, for example, is housed in a tent, a symbol of a wandering people.

Standing back from the story, and looking with the eyes of an historian, it is possible to see how Torah relates to the emergence of Israel as a distinct people, or nation, during Israel's early history. It identifies and values the people's nomadic and tribal roots. It provides an account of how they came to settle in Canaan, the Promised Land, but also a justification of their right to be there. It enables them to see themselves as the covenant people of the God of Israel, through the medium of story. It is, therefore, both an account of Israel's experience and a way of finding meaning in that experience (Bigger, 1989, pp. 83–84). At the end of the chapter there will be the opportunity to consider this further, to explore different perspectives on the Old Testament as reflection on Israel's experience. But now it is time to begin engaging with the text itself.

EXERCISE
📖 **Read (out loud if possible) Exodus 19 to 24.**

Drawing on the information provided below, examine these issues:
- What is your initial reaction? What strikes you, touches you, speaks to you?
- What story is told? Draw on what was learnt about stories in chapter 2: Who is the story about? What sort of story is it, and how is it told? Why might it have been told?
- What different things might the story mean for people in the various contexts in which it has been retold (for example, for Jews in Israel, or in exile, for Jewish Christians in the first century, for Christians today)?
- What has the narrative to say about God, about seeing God and what that does to people, about knowing God and what that means for people?
- What does the story mean for you in your context? How does it relate to your story? Might this help you see God in your situation differently?

## Exodus

This text has some claim to be central to an understanding of Torah. There are a number of links between the passage and what was said above about Torah, in relation to Israel's story, the covenant, worship, and codes found in narrative frameworks.

The setting is the exodus journey from Egypt, at the point at which the Israelites have reached Mount Sinai. The occasion is the ratification of the covenant between God and Israel. At the heart of this occasion is a meeting between God and the people.

In chapter 19 the build-up to the meeting with God is narrated. Chapters 20 to 23 (ending at verse 19) contain the code which is at the heart of the covenant. The end of chapter 23 (verses 20–33) looks forward to the continuing journey to the Promised Land. Chapter 24 relates how the covenant was ratified at a meal shared by the leaders of Israel and God.

The instructions in chapters 20 to 23 fall into two sections. The beginning (20:1–17) is the Ten Commandments or Decalogue (literally 'ten words'). The rest (20:22 to 23:19) represents a series of judgements on particular areas of life. The Ten Commandments set out root principles for God's covenant people. The way of behaving put forward here has parallels amongst other peoples of the Ancient Near East, but certain things stand out: first, the form is distinctive as injunctions ('you shall not ...'); second, the Israelites are not to have many gods, like their neighbours, but just one God; third, the behaviour advocated should flow from the covenant relationship but it is also the test of whether that relationship is working and will continue. The Ten Commandments are also to be found in Deuteronomy 5:1–21. The judgements which follow the Ten Commandments are in the more usual ancient form, that is when X happens, the consequence is ... This has the feel of case law, or precedent, about it. Nonetheless, both sections of the material have common concerns: relations with God and provisions for worship; relations with other people; relations with property, including animals.

The story of the ratification of the covenant is dramatic. God, the creator, comes down to his people in cloud, smoke and fire. As on other mountains in the Bible, God is present on Mount Sinai. This is an encounter with the 'holy'. People eat with God ... and live! It is an archetypal account of a particular dimension of the human experience of God. But it is also a very specific event in the life of the Israelite people, one of the foundation stones of their identity. With other episodes in the exodus narrative, the account of what happened at Sinai has been told and retold by Jews of every generation since as a reminder of their election as God's people. It has been recounted almost as a foundation charter, and it has been recalled in Israel, by Jews in exile, and in every part of the world to which Jews have been dispersed.

## The Prophets: the word of the Lord

As indicated above, the prophets, in Jewish reckoning, include two groups: the Former Prophets (Joshua, Judges, 1 and 2 Samuel, 1 and 2 Kings); and the Latter Prophets (Isaiah, Jeremiah, Ezekiel and the 12 'minor' prophets). The Former Prophets address the period of Israel's history which runs from the conquest of Canaan, through the period of the Judges and the establishment of the kingdom of Israel, to the glory days of David and Solomon, and beyond to the division of Israel into two kingdoms (Israel in the north and Judah around Jerusalem) and the conquest of both. The prophets include such figures as Samuel, Elijah and Elisha. There is some overlap with the period addressed by the Latter Prophets, whose words relate to the latter days of Israel and

Judah, and then to the exile in Babylon and the plight of the remnant left in Judah.

The responsibility of the prophets was to act as mediators between God and God's people, particularly to remind the people of their call to be faithful to God and to the covenant. The prophets spoke the word of God, the word which once spoken cannot be unsaid and which, being the word of God, will come to fulfilment. Feared by kings, often at odds with the people, despised for speaking the truth, the prophets' calling was often a lonely one, and sometimes dangerous. (Read the account of Elijah's flight from Jezebel in 1 Kings 19.) Often the prophets were called to disillusion people, whether it was Samuel pointing out just what having an earthly king would mean for Israel (1 Samuel 8), or the later prophets pointing to the inevitability of Israel or Judah being conquered.

A key difference between the Former and the Latter Prophets is in the genre and style of the books. The books which come under the heading of the Former Prophets are historical in tone and speak about the prophets among many other things. The books of the Latter Prophets are mostly just that: the words of the prophets themselves, their oracles and accounts of how they followed their calling. The oracles of the Latter Prophets develop a message of judgement on Israel and Judah, of the impending Day of the Lord. But also on the other side of that judgement, they offer a message of hope and restoration.

Again, by standing back from the text, by looking at the role of the prophets, we can see them as interpreters. They were steeped in the stories of the Israelite people, and therefore able to see the reality of their present context. They interpreted the tradition in relation to the changing circumstances of the people of the covenant. Faithful to the God of Sinai, but also deeply realistic about human nature, they had a particular gift for seeing things from a different angle or in a new way. Often standing on the edge of society, they spoke of things which were central to the very existence and identity of the people.

---

**EXERCISE**

📖 **Re-read (out loud if possible) Amos 7 and 8.**

Revisit the work you did on Amos in chapter 3. Drawing on the information provided below, examine these issues:    ▶▶

- What is your first reaction to these chapters?
- What can you discover of the different stories told here, for example, Amos' own story, the story of Israel as seen through the eyes of different people, God's story?
- What do you make of the way Amos puts his message across in this passage?
- What has Amos to say about the way we see life and God in these chapters?
- How does what you have learnt relate to what you see in your own context? How does it relate to your story? Do you identify with the prophetic calling?

### Amos revisited

We encountered Amos in chapter 3 as the shepherd turned prophet. As you will recall, he prophesied in the middle of the eighth century BCE, in the time of the two kingdoms of Judah and Israel, although Amos' words were directed towards the latter. Both kingdoms were enjoying a period of prosperity, although the end of the northern kingdom (in 722 BCE) was not far away.

Chapters 7 and 8 of Amos set out a series of visions, together with their interpretations. The images of locusts gathering in early summer and of fire are ones of destruction, about which God relents at the request of Amos. Despite this respite, however, destruction is inevitable; for Israel has been tested, as a wall is tested by a builder with a plumb line, and found to be out of true. A further image comes to represent, for Amos, the end of Israel: the basket of fruit gathered at the end of the summer. In the Hebrew there is a pun here (as well as a vision of approaching autumn), for the word for 'summer fruit' and that for 'end' look very similar. As in a parable, the ordinary things of life seen from a different angle may reveal the word of God.

Amos 8: 4 to 6 reveals the reason for the forthcoming judgement and destruction: the people, while outwardly religious (observing the sabbath and the new moon festivals) lack righteousness. As Amos sees all too clearly, they are oppressing the poor, making profits at their expense. The consequence is to be the coming of the Day of the Lord (8:9–10): but this is to be feared rather than welcomed. Further, there will be a famine, not of food but of the word of the Lord (8:11–14). The consequence for Amos of seeing and saying these things is that Amaziah, priest of the shrine at Bethel, accuses him of conspiracy and tells Amos to go and prophesy elsewhere, in Judah from which he came originally (see 7:10–17).

## The Writings: the wisdom of Israel

The Writings include an assortment of texts which come originally from a variety of dates. There are several ways of dividing them up, but the way indicated earlier in the chapter serves at least to indicate differences of genre and purpose.

### 1 and 2 Chronicles, Ezra-Nehemiah, Daniel

These are broadly historical works. Much the same period is covered by 1 and 2 Chronicles as is covered by 2 Samuel and 1 and 2 Kings: the death of Saul to the fall of Jerusalem. However, it is clear that Chronicles looks back at this period from the time after the exile in Babylon (see 1 Chronicles 9; 2 Chronicles 36:22–23). Ezra-Nehemiah (the two works go together) addresses directly the period after the exile, beginning with the return of the exiles to Jerusalem and Judah. Daniel tells of the period of the exile, although it seems likely that it was written much later.

A major concern, once again, in these works is to understand why the events which happened to the people of Israel and Judah took place, in the context of their relationship with God. Identity, particularly as a subject people within the Persian empire, was a key question. Thus, for example, Ezra-Nehemiah focuses on the rebuilding of Jerusalem and especially of the Temple. Observance of the sabbath becomes a mark of Jewish identity in this period. Ezra-Nehemiah makes it clear that to retain their identity as a people Jews should avoid mixed marriages. And throughout 1 and 2 Chronicles and Ezra-Nehemiah lists of names and genealogies are included as a way of establishing people's roots and identity. Daniel, which has links with earlier prophetic writings and later apocalyptic works (which look forward to a dramatic revelation of God), also addresses the question of what it means to be Jewish, not least through Daniel's insistence on worshipping only God (despite the threat of being thrown into the lions' den in Daniel 6).

### Psalms

The Psalms are not easily dated, except where they refer to particular events (such as exile, in Psalm 137:1). It is likely that they come from different times, even if they were collected together after the exile. They address the whole gamut of human experience in relation to God. Originating in temple worship, they came to play a distinctive role in the worship of the Jewish synagogue and of the Christian church.

## Wisdom writings

The wisdom writings include the books of Proverbs, Job and Ecclesiastes (also mentioned below), as well as the apocryphal works, the Wisdom of Solomon and Ecclesiasticus. Like the Psalms, wisdom writings address the deep questions of human existence and the nature of God. Thus, for example, Job addresses the question of whether one can justify the behaviour of God in the face of innocent suffering. Unlike the Psalms, however, there is an instructional character about wisdom writings. They give guidelines for living.

## The five 'Megilloth' (or 'Scrolls')

These works (The Song of Songs, Ruth, Lamentations, Ecclesiastes, Esther) are a diverse group, brought together because of their later use. Each of them is associated with a particular festival in the Jewish liturgical year (Bigger, 1989, chapter 14).

---

**EXERCISE**

📖 **Read (out loud if possible) the Book of Ruth.**

Drawing on the information provided below, examine these issues:
* How do you react to the main character in the story, Ruth?
* Why did the story become important for the Jews? (See Ruth 4:13–22.)
* Why do you think this story about Ruth, a woman and a foreigner, is included in the Hebrew scriptures?
* What does Ruth's statement in 1:16–17 have to say about God?
* Are there connections to be made between Ruth's story and your own? Which of the characters do you identify with?

---

## *Ruth*

Set in the period of the Judges, soon after the Israelites settled in Canaan, the story of Ruth is an intimate one. It is an unlikely candidate, at first sight, to be included in the Bible. But even family stories can address important questions about humanity.

Ruth is a Moabite. She comes from a people who were despised by the Israelites because they had not helped them on the journey from Egypt (Deuteronomy 23:3–6). Yet she is also a 'stranger' in the land of Israel, and Israelites have a duty towards such people. Caring for the stranger is a mark of righteousness, as is caring for the orphan and the widow. And indeed behaviour towards Ruth goes as far as could be expected towards a stranger: she is fully accepted into the Israelite community as Boaz' wife.

However, Ruth does not simply receive this care passively. She initiates what happens, in her choice to return with Naomi and to accept her people and her God. Even with Boaz, Ruth takes the initiative in approaching him. Out of Ruth's initiative and her acceptance by Boaz comes a son who was to become the grandfather of David.

It is perhaps for all these reasons that Ruth, stranger and woman though she be, is remembered as an important character in the history of Israel. Her story is told at Shavuoth (the Festival of Weeks), and she finds a place too in the genealogy of another key Jewish figure, in Matthew 1:5.

## The Old Testament seen through different eyes

### Through exilic eyes

The usual way of studying the Old Testament has been to begin at the beginning, to explore the origins of the Jewish people and then work forward through their history from there. But this is only one way of understanding the identity of God's people Israel. Another possibility is to look backwards. For example, we can look through the eyes of a Jew in exile in Babylon in the sixth century BCE, at about the time when the Old Testament was being drawn together. From this perspective, the story of Israel and God becomes a way of comprehending the situation of exile, of what had gone wrong with the covenant relationship, and of exile as judgement. It becomes an exploration of whether and how the Jews could 'sing the Lord's song in a strange land' (Psalm 137:4). It leads into the contemplation of hope in exile, of whether there could be a return to the Promised Land, a new exodus.

### Through the eyes of the first Christians

Both the perspectives on the Hebrew scriptures indicated above are rather different from that of first-century Christians, for these Jewish

Christians saw the Old Testament in a new light. As we shall see in the next chapter, the Old Testament became a way of interpreting the new experience of their encounter with Jesus. The familiar texts were pressed into service as they sought to articulate the first answers to the question: Who is this Jesus?

### Through our eyes

In the present century it has become apparent to many Christians that one cannot simply approach the Old Testament via the New Testament. Partly this is a matter of understanding the New Testament better. It has become clear that the Old Testament is one of the keys to understanding the New Testament, but only by being as familiar with the Hebrew scriptures as were the Christians of the first century can we understand the relationship between the two Testaments. To understand the Old Testament in relation to the New Testament, one first needs to understand it in its own right. This is one argument for understanding the distinctiveness of the Old Testament, but there are others.

There is the realisation that the Hebrew scriptures are sacred texts for those of other faiths today, the Jews and the Muslims. Knowing the texts, therefore, is part of understanding the views of different religions in our pluralistic society, and may be the basis for dialogue with those of other faiths.

All this is a reminder of the breadth of meaning in the Old Testament, that it speaks with its own voice (or voices) to people in many different situations. As they reflect on their own situation in the light of the texts, so new things may be revealed. The interpretation of the Old Testament in the pages of the New Testament needs, therefore, to be set on the wider canvas. The fulfilment of God's purposes in Jesus Christ needs to be located in the larger narrative which tells of the God who created the heavens and the earth, and of God's relationship with humanity.

---

EXERCISE

The three texts (Exodus 19 to 24, Amos 7 and 8, Ruth) which have been the focus of the exercises in this chapter represent very different ways of telling stories, of engaging with context, and of arriving at new ways of seeing and knowing. What have you learnt from them about the different ways in which the Old Testament can contribute to the enterprise of living theologically today?

---

# Further reading

Bigger, S (ed.) (1989), *Creating the Old Testament*, Oxford, Blackwell.

Charpentier, E (1982), *How to Read the Old Testament*, London, SCM.

Coggins, R (1990), *Introducing the Old Testament*, Oxford, Oxford University Press.

Dennis, T (1991), *Lo and Behold! the power of Old Testament storytelling*, London, SPCK.

Drane, J (1987), *Introducing the Old Testament*, Tring, Lion.

Rogerson, J (ed.) (1983), *Beginning Old Testament Study*, London, SPCK.

# 6. WHO DO YOU SAY THAT I AM?

## Introduction

In this chapter our attention turns to the New Testament as a response to the crisis of Jesus of Nazareth. This will involve looking at the way the new stories relating to Jesus are woven together with the older stories of Judaism, and at how stories from the Old Testament are seen to be fulfilled but also transformed by Jesus. This will enable us to think about the way the New Testament, through the Gospels and letters, reveals new ways of seeing and knowing God as it seeks to discover answers to two questions: Who is Jesus? Who are we in the light of who Jesus is?

---

*Reflecting on experience*
What is the importance of the New Testament to you?

What do you think you might gain through studying it?

What do you think you might lose?

Which New Testament texts are most important to you? Do you want to start by considering these, or leave them until later?

Which texts do you not know much about? How might you benefit by looking at these?

---

## The New Testament

Chapter 5 involved an exploration of the Old Testament as, in part, a quest for identity formed in different contexts. One aspect of the

Hebrew scriptures is the answers they give to the question: Who are we, God's people?

The New Testament, too, addresses questions of identity but the new situation in which those questions are asked is brought about not primarily by the events of the first century, but by the existence of one person, Jesus of Nazareth. Jesus is the crisis which precipitates a new search for identity. Crisis is the appropriate word, for its Greek meaning is 'judgement'. As the Gospels make clear, people found themselves required by the presence of Jesus to make judgements: about themselves and their relationship with God, and about life and their participation in it. A key question in the New Testament is, therefore: Who are we, who have encountered Jesus? But to answer that question, the New Testament writers had first to discover some answers to a prior question: Who is Jesus? This is the question posed by Jesus himself to his disciples, then and now: 'But who do you say that I am?' (Matthew 16:15) Understanding, or at least grappling with, Jesus' identity comes first. It may lead to an understanding of ourselves.

Grappling with who Jesus was and is involved the early Christians in telling stories. They retold the stories which Jesus had told them. They gathered stories about Jesus. All this did not take place in a vacuum, but rather in the cultural context of the first century. Christianity began as a movement within Palestinian Judaism and spread around the shores of the Mediterranean, often through existing Jewish networks, but also touching Gentiles. And although it became separate from Judaism and ultimately a religion in its own right, first-century Judaism provided the language for the stories.

More than this, intertwined with the stories which were from and about Jesus were older stories. As they reflected on their experience of Jesus, the first Christians did so in the light of their existing scriptures, which were to become known as the Old Testament. In the process, the early church discovered new meaning in the Hebrew scriptures which cast light on Jesus. They found new ways of seeing and knowing God. The revelation of God in Jesus began to be realised in these reflections. It was articulated in what was to become known as the New Testament, which was the record of a new encounter with the God of Israel in his Son, Jesus Christ.

This chapter will provide the opportunity for an exploration of this process in the Gospels and the letters which make up the bulk of the New Testament. But first, a particular example will be examined of the way in which the early Christians found new meaning in older traditions, as a result of the encounter with Jesus.

## The resurrection of Jesus: a way of saying who Jesus is

One of the most surprising encounters with Jesus was the one that took place after his death on the cross. The stories of this encounter speak of an empty tomb, of directions from angels, and of Jesus appearing to his disciples (at the tomb, in Jerusalem, on a road, in Galilee). There are different ways in which this encounter is described in the New Testament. Much of the language, for example, has to do with 'seeing' Jesus. In John 20:18, Mary Magdalene rushes to the disciples and says, 'I have seen the Lord'. But a key statement found in the accounts is that Jesus has risen, or been raised.

Resurrection is so much a part of Christianity that it can often be taken for granted, but what did the first Christians mean by saying that Jesus had been raised from the dead? The answer to this question lies in part in first-century Judaism. In this context the language of people being raised from the dead by God was already becoming familiar. Although resurrection was scarcely to be found in the Old Testament (with the exception of Isaiah 26:19 and Daniel 12:2), a number of Jewish texts which come from the period between the Old Testament and the New Testament spoke of it. At first the hope was that those who died as martyrs would be brought back to life, as a matter of justice. Subsequently, the hope emerged that people would be raised from the dead at the end of the age. Sometimes the hope was that the righteous would be raised by God, sometimes that both righteous and un-righteous would be raised, before judgement took place and people entered into life, or condemnation. Resurrection became part of the Jewish picture of the end, the *eschaton*.

So for early Christians to say that Jesus had been raised was more than a statement about his being alive. It was also to say that it was God who had raised him, and that the end of the age had already happened, at least in the case of Jesus. Further, it was to say that the judgement had already begun in Jesus; the crisis was here and now. For the disciples, the encounter with the risen Jesus made sense of the existing Jewish belief in resurrection but it also radically changed that belief, bringing what had been a future hope into the present.

Each of the Gospel writers reveals something more of what this belief in the resurrection of Jesus might mean. For Mark, what follows is that those who have faith should look forward to Jesus coming again to complete what he had begun. For Matthew, it means that Jesus' followers must make disciples of all the nations. For Luke (writing in the Gospel and in the Acts of the Apostles) the consequence is that the disciples become witnesses to the resurrection, offering people the chance to repent and turn to Jesus. For John, the implication is that those who believe in Jesus have already entered eternal life, having passed beyond judgement.

---

**EXERCISE**

📖 **Read (out loud if possible) Mark 16:1–8.**

In the light of the above, address the following questions:
- Can you think of reasons why the women might have been afraid?
- If their response was frightened silence, what might yours have been?

---

## The Gospels: ways of understanding who Jesus is

The word gospel, or rather its Greek equivalent (*euangelion*), is used in the letters of Paul. It means 'good news', and is used specifically of the good news about Jesus Christ. The word has the same meaning in Matthew but Mark appears to use it as the title for his work. Thus Mark 1:1 reads: 'The beginning of the gospel of Jesus Christ'. It has come to be applied to the four Gospels: Matthew, Mark, Luke and John.

But what are these Gospels? Are they a distinct genre? It now seems clear that in one sense their literary form was not a new one. Richard Burridge (1992) demonstrates that they resemble the lives of heroes, a genre common in the Graeco-Roman world. On the other hand, they are told for a distinct purpose, not simply to relate the life of the hero Jesus of Nazareth, but to enable and encourage belief in Jesus Christ. They are directed towards this end, and it is this that makes them gospels, good news.

Many reasons have been suggested for their being written. We can be reasonably sure that they were written in the period between 65 CE and the end of the first century CE. They draw on earlier, probably oral, sources such as collections of parables or sayings of Jesus. Some have suggested that they were written down because eye-witnesses to Jesus were dying out. Others would suggest that the events surrounding the fall of Jerusalem in 70 CE played a part in encouraging the Gospel writers. Connected with this, and another plausible reason for writing, was the split between Christianity and Judaism in the aftermath of Jerusalem's destruction. For some the Gospels were written for the benefit of the writer's own community; for others they were written to be shared with those outside the community (Bauckham, 1998). Perhaps all these were factors contributing to the emergence of the Gospels, which certainly became central to the identity of the new Christian church.

Those who study the Gospels have also long puzzled over the relationship between them. John is rather different in style and content from the other Gospels but the three synoptic Gospels (Matthew, Mark and Luke) are clearly connected and draw on similar material. Although still challenged from time to time, the usual solution to the 'synoptic problem' is that Mark was written first and was drawn on by both Matthew and Luke. In addition, Matthew and Luke draw on other material which they both knew about but Mark did not. This 'source' is deduced from a study of Matthew and Luke, and does not exist as a document. It consists mainly of sayings of Jesus, and is usually referred to as 'Q' (from the German *Quelle*, meaning source). Finally, Matthew and Luke appear to have drawn on material which was known only to each one of them.

Reading the Gospels side by side raises a question about how we react as theologians to the fact that there are four of them, especially when it is recognised that as well as similarities there are differences, even contradictions between them. One approach is to seek to harmonise, to distil a single picture from the four. This may undervalue the distinctiveness of each Gospel. Valuing the diversity of the four works, on the other hand, may allow us to see them as providing complementary perspectives on the good news of Jesus Christ. This was the approach taken with regard to resurrection above. Amongst other things, it enables us to relate to the different perspectives or stories of Jesus, and to explore how they arise in response to different contexts, revealing particular ways of seeing and knowing God in Jesus.

---

**EXERCISE**

  📖 **Read (out loud if possible) John 4:1–42.**

Drawing on the information provided below, examine these issues:
- How does the Gospel writer interweave the story of Jesus and the story of the Samaritan woman?
- Why might a story about a Samaritan woman be important, for Christians in the first century and for Christians today?
- What connections can you make between this episode and the Old Testament texts which you explored in chapter 5?
- What does the woman discover about wells and water?
- What does she see in Jesus and discover about the consequences of knowing Jesus?
- What are the points of contact between the woman's story and yours? How might this change you?

---

## The Samaritan woman

This episode in John's Gospel sets out to challenge the reader. It focuses on a conversation between Jesus and a woman who was also a Samaritan. The conversation in Jewish eyes would have been unusual (to say the least!) on two counts. Jewish men did not strike up conversations with strange women, and Jews did not talk with Samaritans. Yet Jesus includes the woman among those who are entitled to hear him, and leads her to faith in him without condemning her. Further, she becomes a missionary to her own people. It is possible that this episode was of particular importance to the community in which John's Gospel was written, which may have included some Samaritan Christians amongst its number. It certainly has things to say about Jesus and his followers, including those excluded by other people.

At the same time there are close links between this passage and the Old Testament. It is Jacob's well at which Jesus meets the woman. The woman looks back to the gift of the well by Jacob as something important to her community. Jesus, however, offers something which Jacob could not offer: the water of life.

Jesus is also portrayed in this episode as being in the prophetic tradition. This is seen particularly in his knowledge of the woman's life history (4:17–18). It may also be revealed in the way Jesus sees the well.

Like Amos before him, Jesus sees the word of God in the ordinary things of life. He sees the well not simply as an opportunity for quenching a physical thirst, but as presenting the chance for the woman and others to recognise and quench their thirst for God. Yet Jesus also transcends the prophetic calling. The woman recognises the possibility that Jesus is the Messiah. The people of her city recognise him as the 'Saviour of the world' (4:42).

A further dimension of the way the episode reveals that earlier traditions need to be re-evaluated is to be found in the discussion about worship (4:19–26). The Jewish tradition was of worship in the temple in Jerusalem. The Samaritans, on the other hand, look to Mount Gerizim (where to this day they sacrifice the passover lambs). For the woman, these represented rival places of worship. Jesus indicates that for those who believe in him worship will not be tied to a place but will be 'in spirit and in truth'. Those from different traditions can worship together in any place.

## The letters: addressing who we are in the light of who Jesus is

There are some 21 letters contained in the New Testament, some of which represent the earliest Christian texts, written before the Gospels. That these first Christian writings should be in the form of letters is not surprising. In the early days of Christianity, pressing issues facing particular communities required a written word from the person who had brought Christianity to them. An expectation of the end, and a sense of the urgent need to bring the Gospel to as many people as possible, presumably also played a part in restricting written communication to this pragmatic form. The opportunity and need for more extended writings (such as the Gospels) had not yet been perceived.

The earliest letters, written by Paul himself, include 1 Thessalonians, 1 and 2 Corinthians, Philippians, Philemon, Galatians and Romans. They take the form of other letters of the first century, usually beginning with a greeting similar to that found in any letter of the time. The letters were probably written in the period 50–60 CE. In addressing specific issues, they give a fascinating insight into the debates and struggles of emerging Christianity: how the church should react to Gentile converts; how the Lord's Supper should be celebrated; the expected behaviour of followers of Jesus. In them is reflected the experience and responses of people trying to live out their new-found faith in Jesus Christ.

The remaining letters seem likely to have come from the period between 70 CE and the early second century. During this period the letter, from being simply a practical means of communication, becomes an accepted form for communicating the faith and addressing general issues relating to church life. Many of the letters appear to have been written in the name of an earlier apostle or leading church figure. This practice of writing in someone else's name was not uncommon at the time, and in the church it served to ensure that the person's teaching continued to be heard.

Towards the end of this period and subsequently, the church began to recognise the authority of these letters and their value for other people who sought to follow the Christian way. Thus the writer of 2 Peter (which probably dates from about 130 CE) commends the letters of Paul, comparing them with 'other scriptures' (2 Peter 3:16). Over the next few centuries the letters became recognised as scriptures, finding their place in the New Testament.

The later letters, as well as the earlier ones, give insights into different periods of the early church's development. Although not a narrative form, the letters give us a window onto the story of the first Christians. In all of them theology is done as people grapple with the implications of who Jesus is for their life together and within the wider society. The result, as in the Gospels, is the emergence of new ways of seeing and knowing God.

---

**EXERCISE**
📖 **Read (out loud if possible) Romans 5 and 6.**

Drawing on the information provided below, examine these issues:
- Whose stories are being told in these chapters?
- How does Paul reshape the Old Testament story here?
- What story is being told about baptism?
- What do the chapters have to say about how we relate to God?
- How do you relate to Paul's message? In particular, how might it help you tell the story of baptism today, perhaps your own?

## Romans

One of the things which Paul does in these chapters is to rewrite the Old Testament story, or rather to show how Jesus rewrites that story. Paul points back to Adam's disobedience (related in Genesis 3) as the origin of our estrangement from God. He speaks of the time before Christ when sin and death ruled. In this context law becomes not something which enables people to relate to God, but rather that which reveals their condemnation. With Christ's death, however, the situation is changed. In place of sin, there is freedom from sin and reconciliation with God. Instead of death there is life. Rather than being condemned, people are justified by faith. In place of the burden of the law has come the free gift of grace and righteousness. Christ becomes the second Adam. His death reverses the effect of Adam's sin.

This argument is of particular importance to Paul himself; it relates to his own story. Born a Jew, trained as a Pharisee in all the intricacies of the Jewish law, Paul had to come to terms with what his new relationship with Jesus meant in relation to his past life. The law and its status was a particular issue for Paul. As C K Barrett (1957, p. 9) points out, Jesus had been condemned by a Jewish court, and had died a death which meant that he was cursed under the law (see Deuteronomy 21:23). Yet his resurrection revealed that this was not the case. The law, at least in this respect, was wrong. Paul's solution to this challenge is to show how through his death and resurrection Jesus transcended the law and made it possible for others to do so too. Paul develops this line of thinking in Romans 7, suggesting that those who believe in Jesus have 'died to the law' (7:4).

But Romans 5 and 6 are not only about how Paul's own story relates to that of Jesus. Through his argument, in the pictures he draws, Paul makes it possible for others to enter into Christ's story. If Jesus' death and resurrection are the point of transition from death to life, then Paul reveals that baptizm is the point at which people enter into that transition. 'Do you not know that all of us who have been baptized into Christ Jesus were baptized into his death? Therefore we have been buried with him by baptism into death, so that, just as Christ was raised from the dead by the glory of the Father, so we too might walk in newness of life' (Romans 6:3–4). This is indeed a powerful piece of symbolism. It is a dramatic articulation of how, in being initiated into the Christian community, people are united with Christ and also enter a new era, one in which 'we have peace with God through our Lord Jesus Christ' (Romans 5:1).

## Encounters, stories and seeing things differently

Much of this chapter on the New Testament has explored how the writings contained in it are, in part at least, a response to the encounter with Jesus. A particular focus has been the way in which the first Christians incorporated earlier stories which they knew from the Hebrew scriptures. They discovered, on the one hand, that Jesus fulfilled the stories, but found, on the other hand, that they had to rewrite the stories in the light of Jesus. In the process of rediscovering their tradition, new ways of living theologically emerged, which supported and articulated something of the identity of the new Christian community. The next chapter will consider how the New Testament tradition itself was re-interpreted as Christians sought to translate it within new contexts, and as they grappled with some of the questions about Jesus which were raised, rather than answered, by the New Testament.

---

EXERCISE

Both John 4:1–42 and Romans 5 and 6 have something to say about how stories need to be rewritten in the light of an encounter. Revisit exercise 2 in chapter 2. Reconsider a significant encounter which enabled you to see your life differently. Write about it in one of the following forms:

- as a narrative which tells the story of the encounter and its effect on you (perhaps like John 4);
- as a letter to a friend which explains the significance of the encounter (perhaps like the letter to the Romans).

---

## Further reading

Brown, R E (1984), *The Churches the Apostles Left Behind*, New York, Paulist Press.

Brown, R E (1997), *An Introduction to the New Testament*, New York, Doubleday.

Charpentier, E (1982), *How to Read the New Testament*, London, SCM.

Chilton, B (1985), *Beginning New Testament Study*, London, SPCK.

Drane, J (1991), *Introducing the New Testament*, Oxford, Lion.

# 7. IN SPIRIT AND IN TRUTH

## Introduction

This chapter looks at the development of Christianity through three particular windows: worship in the early church; the development of creeds; and the emergence of the New Testament as an agreed body of Christian texts. The concern is with how Christians went on grappling with identity-shaping questions. As in the New Testament period, it will be seen that the church continued to explore who Jesus was, particularly in relation to God and humanity. Christians were also trying to discover how best to tell the Christian story within their own culture, so as to make sense of their own stories.

---

### Reflecting on experience
As a way of preparing to look at how the early church explored its distinctive identity within the cultural setting of its time, look at a creed (or other historical statement of faith) or a form of worship which originates with a previous generation (for example, *The Book of Common Prayer*). Consider the following:
- What is the importance of the text for you personally?
- How do you think it might relate to the culture in which it originated (in terms of its language, ideas or emphasis)?
- Which bits of the text make sense today, and which do not?

---

## Christianity in the period after the New Testament

As was indicated at the end of the last chapter, exploring the meaning of the encounter with Jesus did not stop at the end of the first century

CE. Indeed it continues to the present day. Further exploration took place as the Christian church grappled with how they might worship and live 'in spirit and in truth'. The stories told by the Christian communities went on developing. New forms evolved for communicating the Christian faith and for articulating the identity of the Christian community.

Partly, this was in response to the texts which had emerged in the first century. What was to become known as the New Testament portrayed Jesus in a number of different ways, thus titles for Jesus abounded: Son of David; Son of Man; Son of God; Messiah; Lord; Saviour of the world; King of the Jews; the Word. All of these contribute to an understanding of who Jesus was and is. But at the same time they raise further questions about Jesus' identity. In particular, who is Jesus in relation to God? And how is this related to Jesus saving humanity?

These questions of belief emerged within the church as it engaged in an on-going process of self-definition. At the heart of the process was the worship of the community, which was rooted in the Christian story, and a retelling of it. The forms of worship, the different liturgies and rites, were central to the church's search for meaning and truth. Of key importance were rites of initiation, centred on baptism. These embodied what was expected of those entering the Christian community, in terms of belief and practice. They gave rise, in part, to the creeds which will be explored in this chapter.

A further dimension of self-definition was the consideration of which texts should constitute the scriptures for the Christian church. Which were to be regarded as sacred and identity-forming? This was a question about the Hebrew scriptures. They had formed the matrix for the Christian texts of the first century, but the question of their continued importance and relevance was a real one. There was also the question of Christian texts. Which were to be regarded as authoritative? This question was at the heart of the process of deciding on the canon of the New Testament, which will be the focus for another section of this chapter.

Part of what initiation rites, creeds and canon were about, was setting boundaries. What (and who) was recognisably Christian, and what (or who) was not? Boundaries of belief and of sacred text embody the boundaries of a religious community. That this is the case reminds us that any process of self-definition, of boundary-setting, does not take place in isolation. It proceeds just as much in relation to those people and beliefs which are beyond the boundary, as in relation to those within. The early church grappled with questions of what it meant to be Christian within the context of the wider society to which they belonged, the Graeco-Roman world.

This world provided language, images and ideas as the medium for articulating the Christian faith. Belief must be communicated in the language of one's own context. It cannot fail to connect with society's way of thinking and living. At the same time the Graeco-Roman world (as with any other subsequent society in which Christianity has been located) presented various challenges to the distinctive Christian identity. The nature of the Christian church was, and is, defined both in relation to society and in distinction from it. This is the creative tension of self-definition.

The outcome of these early centuries of Christian history was, once again, new ways of knowing God, particularly as Trinity, one God in three persons.

## Liturgy: worshipping and belonging

The New Testament gives only hints as to the nature of Christian worship in the first century. There are descriptions of the first Christians participating in Jewish worship (for example, Luke 24:53). There are also indications of how the Christian church was beginning to discover its own identity through distinctive worship. Thus in Matthew's Gospel the word *ekklesia* (usually translated as church) is used, instead of synagogue, suggesting a new worshipping assembly. Throughout the New Testament we have references to baptism as the rite of initiation for new Christians, and to the argument about whether circumcision should continue to be important. The eucharist finds its roots in the accounts of the Last Supper and in passages such as 1 Corinthians 11:17–34 (which was examined in chapter 3). But this does not represent a coherent account of worship; nor does it include orders of service!

Rather more information emerges in the second and third centuries, from descriptions of acts of worship and other references. These include the writings of Justin Martyr (Rome, c.165), Tertullian and Cyprian (North Africa, third century). A particularly important text is the *Apostolic Tradition of Hippolytus*, which will be considered shortly. Those who study liturgy now recognise that worship in these centuries was diverse. There was perhaps some commonality in the shape and structure of liturgy, but there were considerable regional variations and room for those leading worship to improvise as the need arose. This continued for a number of centuries until the need to set boundaries in belief resulted in rather greater standardisation of forms of worship.

---

**EXERCISE**
&#x1F4D6; **Read (out loud if possible) the eucharistic prayer of Hippolytus set out below.**

Drawing on the information provided below, examine these issues:
- What stories are told in the prayer, and how are they told?
- How does the prayer connect with the New Testament? How does it bring the New Testament story into the present?
- How does the prayer focus the relationship between those who celebrate the eucharist and God?
- How might it change your perception of the eucharist to think of the eucharistic prayer as an exercise in story-telling?

---

## Prayer of Hippolytus

After the kiss of peace, the deacons present the bread and wine at the holy table, and the bishop, laying his hands upon the gifts, begins the eucharistic prayer, accompanied by the presbyters who celebrate with him.

> The Lord be with you.
> And with your spirit.
> Lift up your hearts.
> We hold them towards the Lord.
> Let us give thanks to the Lord.
> It is worthy and right.

> We give thanks to you, O God, through your beloved servant Jesus Christ, whom in the last times you sent to us as saviour and redeemer and messenger of your will; he is the Word inseparable from you, through whom you made all things, and on whom your favour rested. You sent him from heaven into a virgin's womb; he was conceived, made flesh and revealed as your Son, born of the Holy Spirit and the Virgin. As he gave full expression to your will, and

created for you a holy people, he stretched out his hands in suffering in order to free from suffering those who put their trust in you. And after he was handed over to suffering, which he freely accepted, that he might destroy death and break the bonds of the devil, tread down hell and give life to the righteous, fix the limit and manifest the resurrection, he took bread, gave thanks to you and said, 'Take, eat; this is my body which is broken for you.' Likewise also the cup, saying, 'This is my blood, which is shed for you; when you do this, do it to remember me.'

We remember therefore his death and resurrection. We offer to you the bread and the cup, giving you thanks because you have accepted us as worthy to stand before you and serve you.

And we ask you to send your Holy Spirit upon the offering of your holy church; to unite all your saints, and to grant them, as they partake, that they may be filled with the Holy Spirit and that their faith may be confirmed in the truth; so that we may praise and glorify you through your servant Jesus Christ, through whom be honour and glory to you, to the Father and the Son with the Holy Spirit, in your holy church, both now and for ages and ages.

As it was, is, and ever shall be, world without end, and for evermore. Amen.

Then follows a series of three brief prayers by the bishop for worthy reception and the true benefits thereof, the deacon directing the people. Then the elevation follows with this dialogue:

Deacon: Let us attend.
Bishop: Holy things to the Holy.
People: One holy Father, one holy Son, one is the Holy Spirit.
Bishop: The Lord be with you all.
People: And with thy spirit.

The people then come forward to receive, after which the service concludes with a prayer and blessing.

The *Apostolic Tradition of Hippolytus* (previously known as the Egyptian Church Order) was identified as being the work of Hippolytus of Rome early in the twentieth century. It is often thought to date from about 215 CE, although there is some debate about this. It may be that included in the version available to us are later alterations and additions. Nonetheless, it contains a mine of information about liturgy in the early church. It includes directions which relate to the worshipping life of a community, and a number of prayers for the eucharist, initiation rites and ordination.

In considering the eucharistic prayer of Hippolytus, Paul Bradshaw (1996, chapter 7) points to the elements of anamnesis and epiclesis as being the oldest parts of the prayer, to which later sections have probably been added. The anamnesis is that section of the prayer in which the saving acts of God are remembered and thanks are given for them. It consists of the paragraph beginning 'We give you thanks, O God ...' This aspect of the eucharist is seen in earlier eucharistic prayers, but also goes back to the practice at Jewish meals which gave rise to the Last Supper. In Jewish tradition this remembrance is such that God's salvation is experienced in the present as the meal is shared. Hippolytus' anamnesis is notable because of its focus on salvation in Christ. In the prayer as we have it, this anamnesis has probably been developed by the addition of a section which relates to Jesus' words at the Last Supper and the clause: 'We remember therefore his death and resurrection, we offer to you this bread and cup.'

The epiclesis, which is also common to earlier eucharistic prayers and Jewish tradition, is the invocation to God to continue his saving acts among his people. It consists of the section of the prayer which begins, 'And we ask you', and continues to the 'amen'. Once again this may include later additions: the request that God send the Holy Spirit, and the reference to Father, Son and Holy Spirit.

The whole prayer provides the opportunity to relive the salvation history of the Christian community, and to look forward to the future fulfilment of that history. It was to be celebrated in expectation of an encounter with the God who had redeemed his people in Christ. Uniting those who break bread with Jesus Christ in the present, it prepared them for the worship of heaven and the fullness of salvation.

## The creeds: believing and belonging

Within the New Testament there are what might be described as 'credal' statements: short summaries, or articulations, of belief in Jesus. In the Gospel narratives these may be found in the mouths of key characters, Peter (Mark 8:29), Martha (John 11:27) and Thomas (John 20:28). In Paul's letters we find a variety of statements, from the succinct 'Jesus is Lord' (1 Corinthians 12:3), to more extensive summaries of Jesus' significance (such as Romans 1:1–6, 1 Corinthians 15:3–8, Philippians 2:5–11). Focusing on Jesus, often on his death and resurrection, such statements communicate the Gospel, the good news, in sound-bite form.

Such summaries of what it means to believe in Jesus Christ continue in later Christian writings, for instance from Ignatius of Antioch in the second century. Particularly in the late second and early third centuries, there emerges a form often known as 'the rule of faith', to be found in the works of such people as Irenaeus, Tertullian and Origen. These seem to represent summaries for various situations of belief in God and in Christ, and sometimes in the Holy Spirit. They appear to have been regarded as setting out the 'apostolic' faith (that is, received from the apostles), and as being authoritative. They could therefore be appealed to in disputes about the faith.

At about the same period (early third century) we also know that those coming for baptism were asked a threefold question (to be found in Hippolytus): Do you believe in God the Father ... Jesus Christ ... the Holy Spirit?

The creeds emerge out of this background of succinct and telling summaries of faith. The first evidence for creeds themselves dates from the mid-fourth century (Young, 1991, p. 3). It is in the form of Lent lectures, which were commentaries on local creeds addressed to those preparing for baptism. Such creeds have a common three-part structure, not unlike that of the Apostles' Creed explored in chapter 2. The setting for these first creeds was a very specific liturgy. Creeds have never entirely lost their liturgical setting, but in the fourth century creeds came to have a wider significance, and became in that period central to the quest for Christian identity. This is particularly the case for the Nicene Creed of 325, and its successor of 381, the Niceno-Constantinopolitan Creed (known today as the 'Nicene Creed' and used in the next exercise). These creeds were the subject of fierce political debate, but would become widely accepted authoritative statements of Christian belief.

---

**EXERCISE**
📖 **Read (out loud if possible) the creed set out below.**

Drawing on the information provided below, examine these issues:
- How is the story told? Look in particular at the way each line encapsulates particular elements of a much bigger narrative.
- What aspects of the language are drawn from Old or New ▶▶

Testament? Which are brought into service for the first time in
order to articulate the Christian faith?
- Do you think people would be led into an encounter with God
  by reading the creed? Or does it work better for those who have
  encountered God in other ways already?
- What part have creeds or credal statements played in your life
  journey?

## *The Nicene Creed*

We believe in one God, the Father, the Almighty,
maker of heaven and earth, of all that is, seen and unseen.

We believe in one Lord, Jesus Christ, the only Son of God,
eternally begotten of the Father,
God from God, Light from Light, true God from true God,
begotten, not made, of one being with the Father.
Through him all things were made.
For us and for our salvation he came down from heaven;
by the power of the Holy Spirit he became incarnate of the Virgin
  Mary, and was made man.
For our sake he was crucified under Pontius Pilate;
he suffered death and was buried.
On the third day he rose again in accordance with the scriptures;
he ascended into heaven and is seated at the right hand of the Father.
He will come again in glory to judge both the living and the dead,
and his Kingdom will have no end.

We believe in the Holy Spirit, the Lord, the giver of life,
who proceeds from the Father and the Son.
With the Father and the Son he is worshipped and glorified.
He has spoken through the Prophets.

We believe in one holy catholic and apostolic church.
We acknowledge one baptism for the forgiveness of sins.
We look for the resurrection of the dead,
and the life of the world to come. Amen.

The belief that Jesus is more than human, that he is in some way divine, may be found in the New Testament. This understanding, that Jesus might somehow be God, sparked off a debate in the early church about how this could be, especially if Christians believed in one God. The Council of Nicaea established the belief that Jesus was not created by God, but 'begotten', that Jesus had existed before creation, and was (the crucial phrase) 'of one being with the Father'. In the Greek the debate was over a single letter (an i, or iota); the Council opted for *homoousios* (of one being), rather than for *homoiousios* (of like being). This sets forth the belief that Jesus is God, in the same way that the Father, the creator, is God. This maintained the oneness of God. It also countered the argument that the creator was inferior to Jesus. This idea was one of the challenges to Christian identity which sprang from patterns of thinking current in the Graeco-Roman world, specifically gnostic thinking.

As well as recognising the divinity of Christ, the New Testament gives a full picture of Jesus' humanity, from birth to death. In the early church there were those who asked how, if Jesus were God, he could also be human. The Council of Nicaea was quite clear that Jesus was human. The creed maintained the belief that Jesus 'suffered death and was buried'. The thinking was that Jesus being human was essential: if he had not suffered and died, he could not have redeemed humanity.

The belief that Jesus was both God and human was, and is, a crucial part of a Christian understanding of God. In the early church period people grappled with this belief in a variety of ways. Some suggested that Jesus was born as a human but subsequently adopted by God, at Jesus' baptism or after Jesus' death. Others suggested that Jesus was God, but subordinate to the Father. Others again agreed that Jesus was God but denied that he had ever become fully human: he had just appeared to those around him to be a human being. All these viewpoints, which were the result of a variety of influences on Christianity, drew back from saying that in Jesus God became fully human. The Council of Nicaea, as we have seen, established the belief that Jesus was both fully human and fully God. This implied that God was fully revealed in Jesus. In Jesus God became fully involved in humanity, and indeed creation. In encountering Jesus, we encounter God's very self.

A further development in understanding which followed the Council of Nicaea was the articulation of a belief that the Spirit was also fully God. This was enshrined in the Niceno-Constantinopolitan Creed of 381. The implication, given that the Holy Spirit also dwells in humanity, is that God is as close to us as the breath we breathe.

In the debate surrounding the Nicene Creed it can be seen how the doctrine of the Trinity emerged in the early church. This is the belief that God is three persons, Father, Son, and Holy Spirit, in one God; that God exists in relationship. But it is also a belief in a God who draws humanity into that communion of being which constitutes God's nature.

## The canon of the New Testament: stories and belonging

Alongside the development of the creeds, over a similar time-span, the church was deciding on what constituted sacred scripture. If the first and second centuries saw a mushrooming of Christian texts, most of which are unfamiliar to Christians today, then it was during the second and fourth centuries that decisions were taken about which texts were authoritative. This was the process which gave us the New Testament.

As indicated in chapter 6, the beginning of this process can be found in one of the latest New Testament texts. 2 Peter 3:14–16 refers to the usefulness of Paul's letters and compares them with 'other scriptures'. This is in contrast to the rest of the New Testament, in which references to the 'scriptures', are to the Hebrew scriptures. Questions about the authority of texts were, however, precipitated by people like Marcion, who wrote in the mid-second century. He wished to abandon the Hebrew scriptures altogether, maintaining that the angry God of the Jews could not be the same as the God of love revealed by Jesus. He also wished to select a very limited number of Christian texts as being definitive, including the letters of Paul and a version of Luke's Gospel.

It was in response to such approaches that Irenaeus, Bishop of Lyons, defended the authority of the four Gospels in about 180 CE. By about 200 CE there exists what is known as the Muratorian Canon, which indicated which texts were to be regarded as having authority. It included texts not known in the modern New Testament, such as the *Revelation of Peter* and the Wisdom of Solomon. It indicated that the *Shepherd of Hermas* might be read in private, but not in public. It did not mention Hebrews, 1 and 2 Peter, or 3 John. Origen, writing in the mid-third century, suggests that the authority of certain texts was disputed: Hebrews, James, 2 Peter; 2 and 3 John, Jude, the *Shepherd of Hermas, Letter of Barnabas, Teaching of the Twelve Apostles, Gospel of the Hebrews.* (He was also among the first to use both the terms Old and New Testament of sacred texts.) At the end of the third century, as is seen in Eusebius, only James, 2 Peter, 2 and 3 John and Jude are disputed. *The Shepherd of Hermas, Letter of Barnabas, Gospel of the Hebrews, Revelation of Peter, Acts of Peter* and *Didache* have all been excluded from the canon. But it was not until the Council of Carthage in 400 CE that the New Testament as it is known today was recognised.

Reflecting on the making of the New Testament canon draws us back into thinking about how the Christian church was involved in setting some boundaries in relation to what was, or was not, recognisably Christian. This boundary setting is also seen in the emergence of creeds and in the evolution of agreed forms of worship. What are modern, living theologians to make of this process?

A particular concern in the early church was with tradition: that which was received from previous generations of Christians to be passed on to others. Several questions emerge out of this concern, which are still important today: Which aspects of tradition reflect a right understanding of the God encountered in Jesus Christ? Which can be relied upon to open up a window onto God for those seeking to understand their present experience? As Christians seek to tell their own stories, with which other stories about God can they be compared? In the second, third and fourth centuries a number of criteria for reliability were used. The early Christians continued to look to the Hebrew scriptures as a guide (while at the same time deciding what should be included in what they came to call the Old Testament). They identified their own sacred texts (the New Testament) from among the Christian writings of the first century, particularly on the basis of what was 'apostolic' (that which could be traced back to those who had known and been sent out by Jesus). They also engaged in reasoned debate and philosophical argument, and they asked what was in keeping with the salvation they knew and experienced in Christ.

At the same time, the debate about what had been received did not prevent the tradition developing. New language was discovered to articulate belief in God (not least that which was discussed at the Council of Nicaea). New forms were found for communicating the faith of the Christian community, in liturgy and in creed. Christians continued to write about their sacred experience. This process continues. New ways of summarising the faith have continued to emerge (the Thirty Nine Articles of Religion, the Westminster Confession, documents from Vatican II, and so on). Liturgy has continued to evolve. Experience has continued to be a test-bed for doctrine, so in the twentieth century, experience of global suffering has called into question the belief that God the Father, being unchangeable, did not suffer when Christ suffered on the cross (previously regarded as orthodox belief). The present generation finds it difficult to believe in a Father who is removed from suffering (Moltmann, 1974).

In the cause of living, worshipping, and witnessing 'in spirit and in truth', those who wish to live theologically must go on bringing the stories of the present and those of the past into dialogue or conversation. Only then will they discover ways of seeing and knowing God in a way that is appropriate to their context.

---

**EXERCISE**

Look around you in order to identify one or more of the following:
• a modern statement of faith (perhaps a hymn or song);
• a form of worship which encapsulates twentieth-century Christian faith.

Consider how each example relates to the Christian faith received from previous generations. Does it confirm, extend, re-articulate, or question the tradition?

---

## Further reading

Bradshaw, P (1996), *Early Christian Worship*, London, SPCK.
Brox, N (1994), *A History of the Early Church*, London, SCM.
Comby, J (1985), *How to Read Church History* (volume 1), London, SCM.
McGrath, A (1997), *Christian Theology: an introduction* (second edition), Oxford, Blackwell.
Young, F (1991), *The Making of the Creeds*, London, SCM.

# 8. TODAY'S WORLD

## Introduction

In order to be able to live theologically, we need to be able to examine and explore our present situation or context. In chapter 4 we argued that a very good way of doing this was to create what we called 'thick descriptions'. However, any thick description will need to take account of the broader contexts in which the situation is set and in which the investigation operates. This chapter will therefore examine what it means to live in a culture that is often labelled 'post-modern' but in which new ways of interpreting the world combine with those that have come from 'modern' and even 'pre-modern' times. It will then investigate the way that we view the cosmos and the issues raised by advances in science and technology.

Alongside that, the chapter will also look at the way that theology is given a key context that comes to us through the scriptures and tradition of the church. This is the perspective provided by the Kingdom of God and the recognition that Christian discipleship and the life of the church are lived out 'between the times', in which we recognise that we are living with a 'new creation' in Christ, but are still awaiting the final fulfilment of humanity and of the whole created order when 'Christ will come again'.

*Reflecting on experience*

When you think about the society in which you live, how does it make you feel?

What features of our culture make you uncertain? Which do you feel you can rely on?

What sort of theology do you think is appropriate within our culture? What are its key features?

## Pre-modern, modern and post-modern

Three ways of describing society are explored in this section. These are *pre-modern*, *modern* and *post-modern*. The term *pre-modern* identifies the period before the industrial revolution of the seventeenth century. The term *modern* refers to the time from the seventeenth to the mid-twentieth century which produced what is often labelled 'Enlightenment' thinking. The term *post-modern* refers to the way that society has developed through the second half of the twentieth century.

Throughout this book we have been talking about the way that stories can help us to 'see' better. The following is a story about Sue who took her twelve-year-old son to the shoe shop to buy trainers. In the shop Sue met several other people who were trying to buy trainers for their children. It was near to the start of term and the cost of being a parent was now weighing heavily on their shoulders.

As far as Sue could tell from the snatches of conversation she could hear and the body language she could see, most of the parents were having a similar problem. Outside the shop were some trainers for £20. Inside the shop similar-looking trainers were £90. As far as anyone could tell the trainers were identical except for the markings on the side. They looked as though they had come from the same factory and had been made on the same last. What was going on here? Most of the parents were trying to encourage their children to buy the £20 trainers.

'Look', said the parents, in their different ways, 'these shoes cost a lot less, we don't have money to burn, have these £20 trainers.' In turn each child was adamant that they needed the £90 trainers. One child was in tears. One child was throwing a wobbly. One was stuck in a corner, sulking.

Sue told her son, 'Look, I don't know what has got into you. Your father and I have always found we can buy good quality shoes without spending a fortune. Don't be so naughty.'

Sue listened to another parent. The father was saying to his daughter, 'Look, these shoes are just as good as the expensive ones. The only difference between the two pairs is the marks, the logo on the side. Be reasonable. Any reasonable person can see they are the same and will therefore buy the cheaper pair.'

One pair of customers was very different. 'Of course you need the £90 trainers,' said the parent, and mother and daughter soon happily left the shop. But the other conversations were not going so well.

Sue turned to look at the last pair of customers. A mother was telling her son, 'I don't understand you. I just do not know how you think at all. I don't understand you.' The son replied, 'No one understands me.'

Theology is often stimulated by crisis, and this was certainly a domestic crisis. It may not be important on the world scene but certainly, for these people at this time, it was a crisis. And the story does tell us much about the crisis that our society is facing at present. Consider the four responses. They tell us about our past cultures as well as our present. In part the responses to the crisis caused by the trainers were letting us see how different societies pass on information about what it means to be human and how we are supposed to behave.

Where does the response, 'I don't know what's got into you?' or 'Don't be naughty' come from? It comes from *pre-modern* society where social information is passed on from one generation to the next. The older generation tells the children, 'This is the way the world is, learn it as we learnt it from our parents. This is what we believe. This is the way we behave. Learn the ways of the family. Learn the ways of our society.' So if the child of a pre-modern society does not conform to the ways of the parents, there are two main possibilities why this should be so. The child is wilfully naughty. We could call this 'sin'. The child would be seen as deliberately going against the ways of the society or family. Or the child could be possessed by an evil spirit. Something has 'got into him' to make him act in this way.

'Be reasonable' comes from our more recent history. The seventeenth century saw the beginning of a process in the West that rejected the old authorities of church and state in favour of a new scientific world-view. With the rise of this 'Enlightenment' thinking came the need to test everything against an objective truth that could be proved by experiment and supported by reasoned argument. This society, highly

influenced by scientific thought and with an unerring belief in the technological progress of humankind, is called *modern*. Modern, used in
this sense, should not be confused with 'current' or 'contemporary' society. The story of the trainers lets us see how the phrase 'be reasonable'
has shaped the way that we think. It comes to us through a time that
demands that we respond to reasoned thinking with a reasoned
response.

So far, then, we have seen two ways in which our society passes on
information. The first says, 'This is the way we do it, learn it because this
is the way we learnt it from our fathers. Trust me, I am your elder.' The
second way says, 'This is the way we do it because it makes sense, we
have the proof, it is reasonable. Trust me, I am an expert.'

But this is not the whole story. The context in which we attempt to
live theologically is even more complex than this. Poor Sue cannot just
turn to the 'father's' way of doing things. Society has changed. Nor can
she just rely on logic to persuade her son. In our society the old ways are
regarded with suspicion. Indeed, we have become highly suspicious of
experts in general because they tell us different things. One expert this
year will be telling us that salt is good for us and next year that it is bad
for us. And we know that experts often have vested interests. For a long
while experts were hired by tobacco companies to tell us that smoking
was entirely safe. We are no longer reassured by 'reasonable' arguments.

Our current society is sometimes labelled *post-modern*. It is characterised by a loss of trust in systems of thought and the experts and
guides who promote them. The old communal certainties are dead and
are being replaced by the belief that, 'The way I see things is just as good
as the way you see things. You have no right to tell me what to think. My
way is just as good as anyone else's.' If this is so, how can we be expected to understand anybody else? 'I just do not understand you', says the
parent. 'Nobody understands me', replies the child.

And probably never before have so many people been given so much
choice: career choice, moral choice, religious choice, lifestyle choice.
And if you do not like your life, or if you do not like your version of
religion, then change it. Become somebody else.

But the story of the trainers lets us see that the child is not in fact free
to choose, to make up his own mind. The pressures from the peer group
to buy only certain brand names appears to be immense. And this, in
turn, is supported by the power of advertising. The brand names of
multi-national companies, producing a wide range of consumer goods,
have become part of our daily lives. Advertising feeds our lifestyle
choices and our sense of self.

We can begin to see how our lives and selves are formed in a very complex interaction of beliefs and behaviour. Following the older generation is only one way in which we make sense of the world. Logic and reason are only part of the way that we make choices. The pressures involved in making individual lifestyle choices are considerable in a world that had, in the recent past, been taught to think in certainties but has discovered that truth is often a matter of perspective. And the church is not immune from these different ways of understanding the world. Like any other social group it contains elements of the pre-modern, the modern and the post-modern. These three aspects are characterised in the book *Tomorrow is Another Country: post-modernism and Christian education* (General Synod Board of Education, 1996) as 'Church of England and Son' (pre-modern), Church of England PLC'(modern) and 'Church of England Enterprises' (post-modern). Church life and ministry, like theology itself, lives and works in a complex cultural situation where older certainties are giving way to competing views of authority and competing ways of understanding the world. The agreed moral framework that Christianity provided in the West for many centuries has broken down into a society characterised by competing claims for truth. 'I just do not understand you', says the parent. 'Nobody understands me', says the child.

---

**EXERCISE**

How would you react to the child? Would you say, 'I don't know what's got into you, don't be so naughty'? Would you say, 'Be reasonable, use a bit of common sense, be logical'? Would you say, 'I just don't understand you'? Or would you react in a different way, or just buy the expensive trainers?

Consider why you would react in this particular way and what understanding of the world is implied by this.

Give other examples of the ways that we use expressions like this to reflect the way that we understand the world.

Identify the challenges and the opportunities that living in a 'post-modern' culture might provide for the church and for living theology.

## The cosmos

This century has seen our knowledge of the universe grow in a dramatic way. The science of the 'Enlightenment' had challenged the belief that we lived on a flat earth with the waters above and below. We were not the centre of the universe and the sun and stars did not revolve around us. Indeed, science in the twentieth century has come to the conservative estimate that there are 1,000 million galaxies in the universe. Our solar system is therefore an insignificant part of what is a little galaxy. The place is huge. Our theology is lived out in this knowledge.

We no longer fully trust our powers of reason to make things better. The technological revolution has made many improvements for life in the West (or North as it is more accurately described). But this same revolution has also brought with it the possibility of destroying the earth that gives us life. It would also appear that as the rich, technologically advanced countries (the North) get richer, the poor countries (the South) get poorer.

We are seeing the fruits of scientists' work in the field of genetics. On the one hand many painful and destructive diseases may be eradicated by this understanding. On the other hand there are many moral issues that are being raised for the first time, for example, designer babies and cloning.

The political map of the world is changing. The breakdown of the Soviet Union has given a new dynamic as new political and economic alliances are being formed. Our places of work are affected by multinational companies and our employment increasingly affected by decisions made in other parts of the world. There is no single global organisation that is in control of the world economy in the way that national economies were once controlled by their governments. The world of work can feel very risky.

The past century has seen the growth of ideas about scripture and the faith that have left many people bewildered. Many of the ideas of modern theology are not taught to ordinary Christians or they are taught badly. But the tradition moves on. Our understandings about our faith are now being shaped by the kinds of questions that were addressed in the previous paragraphs. And as we saw in chapter 1, our faith and theology are also being shaped by influences from liberation theology, from a feminist critique of gender and power, and by our continuing debate about what it means to be a human being.

As we saw in chapters 5 and 6, our scriptures were written in a pre-scientific world context and we therefore need to have this in mind as we search for truth. We also need to bear in mind that for nearly 2,000 years the Bible has been interpreted for us by white, 'middle class', European males. There is nothing wrong with being white, male and middle class, or with having a scientific world-view, but we now recognise that these 'positions' have affected the way that we have seen and interpreted the scriptures. So again, we need to be aware of these and other perspectives when examining our faith and our scriptures.

In the face of this uncertainty and sense of risk, some people turn to a form of fundamentalism. Fundamentalism is the belief in a set of ideas that are held to be true for all time and cannot be challenged. Scripture, for example, is seen to be utterly true in every respect, and must not be questioned. In fact, different groups of fundamentalists believe hugely different things about their faith and about scripture. In the end to revert to fundamentalism is to subvert the process of living theology.

In the face of risk and uncertainty some people turn to experience. 'If I experience something it must be true. Only experience is the test of reality.' But those outside this experience may be able to point out inconsistencies. And so experience on its own will not be sufficient; we are again called to live theologically in a complex and often difficult arena.

---

**EXERCISE**

This section has explored some of the changes that are happening in our day. List some other changes, particularly as they affect your life.

How do these changes in our knowledge and understanding of the world affect the way that we live and work out our faith? What are the challenges and the opportunities?

---

## Thy kingdom come

As we recognised in chapter 6, the New Testament bears witness to the belief that, with the resurrection of Jesus from the dead, something new has happened in the history of humanity. For the first Christians, encountering the risen Christ gave substance to the hope that a new age had begun and for St Paul, Christ's resurrection inaugurates a 'new

creation' (2 Corinthians 5:17). It enables believers to live in the knowledge that death, the dominant feature of the present age, has finally
been overcome. Yet St Paul also recognised that to live in this new
creation is to live with a tension. Although the new creation has come
into being, the ultimate transformation of all creation is still in the
future.

This tension is present in the way that the Gospel writers understand
the Kingdom of God. The Kingdom provides a key context in which the
'good news' of Jesus was proclaimed and in which Jesus' role is understood. When Isaiah looked forward to a time of hope and deliverance
for Israel, he imagined God establishing a kingdom of justice and righteousness. This would be overseen by an earthly king of the house of
David. Such a kingdom was understood to be very much within the
bounds of human history. However, later on, and partly through their
experience of conquest at the hands of successive world powers, this
hope changed for the Jews. As the apocalyptic tradition developed in
Israel, so God's kingly rule was seen to lie beyond history and was to be
established by a dramatic inbreaking into the present world order. God's
agent in this process was popularly assumed to be the Messiah. Therefore Jesus' preaching about the Kingdom, or perhaps more accurately
the kingly rule of God, and the way that the first Christians understood
the nature of his messiahship, are very significant for understanding
him and his work of salvation. To this end the Gospel writers all bear
witness to the way in which Jesus' messiahship grew from his special
relationship with God, was shaped by his suffering and fulfilled through
his death on the cross. Their understanding of the Kingdom was therefore formed by the manner of Jesus' life and death as well as through the
content of his teaching.

As the New Testament writers all recognised, there is a huge tension
at the heart of the image of Kingdom. Pictures of the Son of Man 'coming in clouds with great power and glory' (Mark 13:26) to establish the
Kingdom in the future are in tension with his proclamation at the
beginning of the Gospel that 'the time is fulfilled, and the Kingdom of
God is at hand' (Mark 1:15). Indeed this tension between a Kingdom
that has dawned with Jesus but is yet still to come in its final consum-
mation permeates the whole of the New Testament and still provides an
important context in which we live and do theology today.

This understanding of Kingdom also gives an important context for
the outpouring of the Holy Spirit in the New Testament. Jewish thought
had long associated the coming of the Holy Spirit with the dawning of

the new age, and St Paul tells the Corinthian Christians that 'it is God who establishes us with you in Christ and has anointed us, by putting his seal on us and giving us his Spirit in our hearts as a first instalment' (2 Corinthians 1:21–22) and further that God 'has given us the Spirit as a guarantee' (5:5). In Romans 8:23 Paul calls the Spirit the 'first fruits'. The first fruits were traditionally the first portion of the harvest to be offered to God and were regarded again as the first instalment or pledge of what was to be finally delivered. The Spirit therefore gives the believer an assurance of their ultimate salvation, a salvation that in-volves not just the individual Christian, but the community and indeed the whole of creation. This understanding of the Spirit gives a context to many who have experienced charismatic renewal in the church in recent decades. This experience has often been described as a moment of encounter with God which supports and confirms their faith while helping them to glimpse what life in God might finally be like.

For Paul, the work of Christ in establishing the Kingdom was essentially one of reconciliation. He therefore explains to the Christians at Corinth that God 'reconciled us to himself through Christ, and has given us the ministry of reconciliation' (2 Corinthians 5:18). To reconcile is to end a relationship of enmity and to be in a 'right relationship' with the other. This right relationship is characterised by peace and goodwill and is a sign of the Kingdom's presence and efficacy. The theologian Paul Tillich (1978, pp. 358ff) believes that this 'right relationship' provides the basis for four signs of the Kingdom. He identifies these as being right relationship with creation, right relationship between individuals, right relationship between groups of people and right relationship with God. This does not mean that Tillich understood the Kingdom of God as something that was realisable in this world, a kind of moral ideal to which human beings must aspire and eventually achieve. He rather saw these signs of the Kingdom as 'first fruits', characteristics that find moments of expression in the life and witness of those who proclaim the Gospel, but will not be known in their fullness until the whole created order finds its fulfilment in God.

The church also lives 'between the times', experiencing the tension that comes from being an institution that is in a sense both human and divine, living in the world yet being an agent of the Kingdom, living as part of society yet called to critique its beliefs and values from a Kingdom perspective. To be part of the church is to live in a community that is called to proclaim the Gospel afresh in each generation. To live theology today is to live within that fellowship and within the tradition from which and through which the story of salvation is told. To live theology is to engage in a dialogue between the scriptures and credal statements of the church and the needs and concerns of the present, and to find outcomes and promote action consistent with the imperatives of the Gospel and the values of the Kingdom. To live theology is to acknowledge the boundaries of faith and the consequences of error. Further, to walk with Christ is always to walk with others, to share a common faith, a common hope, a common love and a common discipline. To be within the body of Christ acknowledges the different but complementary gifts and ministries of others under the headship of Christ, to live for the Kingdom and to wait for its fulfilment.

---

**EXERCISE**
How does our knowledge and understanding of the Kingdom of God affect the way that we live and work out our faith?

What does it mean to live theology in the tension between the 'now' and the 'not yet'?

---

**EXERCISE**
📖 **Read (aloud if possible) Matthew 5:13–16.**

Explore what it means to call the Christian community 'light' and 'salt' in today's society.

Examine the following models that are used for the church and explore what each one says about:
• the nature of the church;
• the role of the church in society;
• the relationship of the church to the Kingdom.

---

## Models of church

Community, sign, elect, family, fellowship, body of Christ, yeast, pilgrims, carers, saved, royal priesthood, witnesses, watchers, stewards, peacemakers, members, people of God, nation's faith, boat, ark, ethical community, faith community, one, holy, catholic, apostolic.

## Further reading

Appignanesi, R and Garratt, C (1995), *Postmodernism for Beginners*, Cambridge, Icon Books.

Bevans, S B (1992), *Models of Contextual Theology*, Maryknoll, New York, Orbis.

General Synod Board of Education (1996), *Tomorrow is Another Country: postmodernism and Christian education*, London, Church House Publishing.

Giddens, A (1990), *The Consequences of Modernity*, Cambridge, Polity Press.

Graham, E (1996), *Transforming Practice*, London, Mowbray.

Grenz, S (1996), *A Primer on Postmodernism*, Grand Rapids, Michigan, Eerdmans.

# 9. TOM'S STORY

## Introduction

In this chapter we will describe an example of living theology by telling Tom's story. You will then be asked to do this activity for yourself. You will recognise from the story that living theology is a process which involves an engagement between the situation that Tom encounters at work and the scriptures and traditions of the faith. This engagement or dialogue, undertaken in the power of the Holy Spirit, suggests an appropriate way forward for Tom. There are no 'right' or 'wrong' answers, only a searching after truth. However there is integrity in the way that Tom and his friends work. The encounter is critical. Tom used an appropriate method of study and his thinking was supported by scholarship.

---

**Reflecting on experience**

In using this book what new things have you learnt about yourself, about theology, about culture, about God?

Have your beliefs and ideas been challenged, or confirmed, or both?

What do you understand, at this point, by 'living theology'?

---

## Tom's story

There is a sense in which all that has been described in this book so far is coming together in Tom's story. In chapter 1 we sketched out the context that gave birth to this method of living theology. In chapter 2 we explored the important part that story-telling has to play in the way that we make sense of the world and pass it on to others. Much of our faith comes to us in story form and much of the way that we understand our own world is the result of the stories that we hear and tell about it. Key to this whole process are the stories that we can tell about ourselves. These stories enable us to express the history that has formed us and given us the values, attitudes and agendas that influence the way we think and act today.

Chapter 3 examined the way in which context informs our understanding of any situation and is basic to any investigation. Contexts give situations their basic shape and form and are key to their understanding. Local and global contexts provide the milieu in which stories are set and in which their interpretation occurs. Chapter 4 explored seeing and knowing and recognised the importance of investigating any situation from a variety of perspectives to feed and support a seeing and a knowing that is Christ-like. The 'thick description' provides a vehicle through which a situation can be investigated, its contexts identified, and an analysis of the different perspectives undertaken. This in turn can help to define what outcomes or actions are appropriate.

In chapters 5, 6 and 7 we turned our attention more fully to our tradition and, informed by modern scholarship, explored how previous generations had been involved in story-telling. This was a way for them, too, of making sense of context, of discovering new ways of seeing God and of understanding what action they should take. Looking at the Old Testament we discovered different genres of writing and explored their relationship to the different contexts in which the Jews found themselves at different points in their history.

In chapter 6 we explored the New Testament as response to the crisis of Jesus. We discovered how new stories relating to Jesus were woven together with older stories. It emerged that, for the first Christians, the encounter with Jesus fulfilled the stories from the Hebrew scriptures but also involved them in rewriting those stories. We considered how a new vision of God in Christ emerged.

Chapter 7 extended the process, examining new ways of articulating belief, new story forms such as creed and eucharistic prayer. We considered how these evolved in response to further questions about who Jesus was and as Christianity found itself in new cultural contexts. We recognised a particular concern in the early church to identify which stories contributed to an understanding of what it meant to be Christian and enabled people to locate their own stories within the Christian story.

Chapter 8 returned to the present and described two further key contexts in which the practice of living theology must take place. The first of these is a society that has been called 'post-modern'. That term is partly a description of what society is like and the agendas that that provides for theology. However, it is also important because post-modernism affects the very way that we work and the methods that we use.

The second context is provided by the Christian community which lives in contemporary society but is an agent of the Kingdom of God. Theology is therefore undertaken with a community that is working out its life and ministry in a post-resurrection world which has still to find its fulfilment in Christ.

## Tom's time of crisis

Tom was a middle manager for a multi-national company. He had responsibility for over 100 people in his office. He worked hard and often spent over twelve hours a day at his work. He was conscientious and he was glad to be in work and to work for a prestigious organisation.

Being a family man, he was worried about the amount of time he spent at work. Tom was also very concerned for his staff. They too worked long hours in order to complete their work. He questioned the way that the firm took up so much of their family time.

Now there was a crisis for Tom. As a manager he had to make ten per cent of his workforce redundant. Twelve people from his department had to lose their jobs. The instruction had come from head office in the USA.

What was Tom to do? He was a Christian, a strong member of his church. He was a house group leader and well thought of, but here he was with sleepless nights, worrying about his job. To whom could he go for advice? How could he live theologically? How could he live out his faith? What was he to do? Tom made up his mind to go to his house group with the problem. They would help him think and pray through this problem.

At the next meeting Tom told them his story. They listened sympathetically, but were not able to help him very much at first. They felt that Tom just had to put up with the situation. It was the way the world was. But someone said, 'Hang on a moment, I'm going to tell the story again. I know what it feels like to be made redundant. I want to tell the story from that perspective.' At that point Tom, as group leader, suggested that each member of the group should write the story from a different perspective, putting the key details on a postcard.

The postcards revealed all sorts of ways of telling the story. There were insights from the world of psychology and sociology. Some insights were from the assumptions that circulated in society. These were the ideas that 'everyone knew to be true'. A couple of the group were trained counsellors and wrote out insights from the world of therapy. Some of the responses were written as if from other characters involved in Tom's story, for example, from the boss's point of view. These responses, written on cards, were placed on the floor so all could see them. The cards sparked off other ideas.

At the end of the evening Tom and the group had identified various ways in which Tom might act, but there was no obvious right answer. Should he resign as a protest and put his own family at risk? Should he just do the job and not think twice about it? After all, this is the way the world is. Should he put forward a case to his bosses for keeping extra staff in his department even though that would mean other departments would have to lose more staff?

Should each person work such long hours and therefore put other people's jobs at risk? Should he set up a business that would try to live outside the dilemma? Did he agree with the bosses' understanding that it was important for the company to remain efficient? The loss of ten per cent of the workforce would ensure the future of the rest of the company.

The group ended with prayer and promised to keep thinking about Tom's problem for the next meeting. In particular, the group promised to think about responses from Christian scripture and tradition. One member of the group had reminded them all of the key question: What difference does it make that Tom is a Christian? They agreed to summarise responses from the Christian story and put those on another set of postcards for next time.

At the next meeting Tom and the group laid out all their cards on the floor. There were quite a number. Some were very similar and were immediately put together. They all provoked discussion.

Some of the cards continued the debate of the previous week. There was a card that read: 'The technique is this: as you make each person redundant give them a bar of chocolate as this will ease their stress.' No one was sure if this card was ironic or not! However, someone was sure the technique actually was encouraged in some management circles. The counsellors offered their services on the cards they wrote but Tom felt that this was not getting to the heart of the issue as it seemed to him that this was a social problem and not a personal one. The evening's discussion continued with some strong debate.

The cards which had responded with scripture were examined. The workers in the vineyard figured largely (Matthew 20). Other cards from scripture were discussed. Another card said: 'The work ethic means we are expected to work hard. If the people made redundant work hard they will find another job. This is the meaning of the parable of the talents in Luke's Gospel.'

The group immediately opened their Bibles to look at the passage (Luke 19:11–27). They then asked the person who had written the card to explain what he meant. He said, 'Well, in the parable the nobleman is God. We are the servants. God asks us to do the best we can with what he gives us.' Someone else said, 'Are you sure that is the way it should be read? What about this verse: "To all those who have, more will be given; but from those who have nothing, even what they have will be taken away." That doesn't sound like the God I believe in.' Another member agreed: 'God telling us to make money doesn't fit with the story of the rich ruler who is told to sell everything and give to the poor. That comes in Luke too, doesn't it?' They quickly discovered that the story was indeed in Luke, and was quite close to the parable of the talents (Luke 18:18–25). It concluded with Jesus saying: 'How hard it is for those who have wealth to enter the Kingdom of God!'

Then the group looked at all the passages which were near the parable of the talents, to try and discover the bigger story that Luke was telling. They found the following: the rich ruler, Jesus' prediction of his death, a beggar who sees, the occasion when Zacchaeus gave half of his possessions to the poor, the parable of the talents, Jesus entering Jerusalem on a donkey, Jesus exposing the temple as a den of robbers. It became clear to them that, in Luke, Jesus is on the side of the poor. As it says in Luke's beatitudes: 'Blessed are you who are poor, for yours is the Kingdom of God' (Luke 6:20).

The group began to think that perhaps the story about the nobleman did not refer to God. It was about the way the world operated, rather than about God's way. In Luke, God appears to be generous to the poor.

The response to Jesus, suggested by the stories of the rich ruler and Zacchaeus, is to give to the poor, not to take away from them. The nobleman is simply a nobleman who acts unjustly. So why did Jesus tell the parable? If it was not to advocate some kind of work ethic, then why? From Luke 19:11 it appears that the parable is told because people were thinking about the Kingdom of God. Was the parable telling them that the Kingdom of God was not like that of the nobleman, who went to grab royal power? Rather, was it like the kingship of Jesus, who rode into Jerusalem riding on a colt, to give up his life?

The discussion that evening was like no other that the group had ever had. Tom felt he was nearing an understanding of his position. Through looking at the Christian story in this new way, he suddenly saw that there were two ways that he might act in the context of his work. He might act according to the way of the world, or he might act in a way that was in keeping with the Kingdom of God. And if he acted in a Kingdom way that meant seeking justice.

But what did that mean in the complexity of Tom's situation? At this point some of the other postcards, relating to the Christian tradition, became relevant. There were cards reminding Tom of the incarnation of God in Jesus and his suffering with his people, especially the poor and dispossessed. Someone had written down an extract from one of the statements of faith they said in church, the Nicene Creed. They had put: ' "For us men and for our salvation he came down from heaven." For me this does not mean "saved from the world", but "saved with the world". Perhaps Tom should try to change the economic system.' This was very much in keeping with another card which drew on the confession used in their church during Holy Communion. It read: ' "Almighty God, our heavenly Father, we have sinned against you and against our fellow men in thought and word and deed, through negligence, through weakness, through our own deliberate fault." I believe we are part of an economic system that does damage to some people and that is why I say the confession with meaning.'

Tom began to see more clearly what he should do. He knew he could not resign. He could not walk away from the situation. He had to continue to be involved, in the way that Jesus was involved. Tom also could not simply go on doing his job, ignoring the injustice. He knew that he had to do what he could, however small, to create a better economic system. Pastorally, he wondered how he could support those who were to be made redundant, particularly in their search for other work. In a more prophetic way, he began to think about talking to his line manager. Although he knew he was taking a risk, he felt that he had to talk to her about his concerns. He also wanted to see whether together they could see the situation in a new light. He resolved as well to search out other people in his organisation, and perhaps outside it, who felt that economics was not simply about profit and efficiency but also about care and justice. Tom knew that he was not going to bring in the Kingdom of God overnight but he also knew that he had to look for signs of the dawning of the Kingdom. And he had to behave and act as though he believed that one day Christ would bring in the Kingdom in all its fullness.

## The significance of Tom's story

Tom's story is all about living theology. We now need to stand back from it in order to discover how Tom and his house group came to see his situation differently.

There were two initial dimensions to their discussion and thinking. They looked at Tom's situation, and they explored the Christian story. In both cases they went through a similar process. As they began to think about Tom's situation, they saw things at first from a rather narrow perspective. As far as they were concerned that was just the way the world was. We might describe this as a 'thin description' of Tom's position. Then they began to tell a variety of stories that helped them to engage with Tom's context more fully. This helped them to see things afresh, as they looked at what was going on from different viewpoints, and as they saw the variety of possible outcomes. All this increased their knowledge of Tom's dilemma. They had arrived at what we would describe as a 'thick description' of a complex scenario.

Similarly, as they focused on insights from scripture and tradition, they started with a narrow view of what was on offer. Their thin description in this area was the accepted view of the interpretation of a parable, that it was about the work ethic. Once again, however, they looked more widely. As they engaged with the stories which surrounded the parable in Luke's Gospel, they began to see the bigger story that Luke was telling. This challenged them to see a fresh meaning in the parable, but also to grow into a deeper knowledge of Jesus and of God. Insights from the tradition then contributed to a thick description of a key aspect of the Christian story: the Kingdom of God.

The creation of two thick descriptions, one relating to Tom's story, the other to the Christian story, resulted in a number of things happening. First, a meaningful dialogue took place involving the two thick descriptions. Connections were made between the two stories in a way that had not been possible before. At the same time, working on seeing from different angles (in two areas) had meant that the group had moved from a closed perspective to a more open one. This openness became an openness to the Holy Spirit. So in the midst of the thick descriptions and the dialogue between them, there was an encounter with the living God. In that moment of revelation Tom and the group learnt that they had been living theologically.

---

**EXERCISE**

It is now time for you to think about your own situation. Is there something at home, at work, in the church or in the community that needs thinking about? Decide on one situation. The aim of the exercise is for you to explore the situation in a similar way to that adopted by Tom's house group as they looked at his situation.

It is possible to do this exercise on your own, using your imagination to see different people's perspectives. If possible you should, however, work with a group, or a friend, so that they can contribute their views. Whether on your own or with others, proceed as follows.

First, engage with the particular situation. Think what your initial thin description of it might be. Then explore a number of different responses to the situation that will help you arrive at a thick description, so that you can see things afresh. Write the key details of the different stories or perspectives on postcards.

Second, engage with scripture and tradition. What is your first point of contact? Next, how might you see the bigger story? Again, the objective is to move from thin to thick description. Record different perspectives on postcards once more.

Third, use the postcards to help you explore the dialogue between the two thick descriptions, those of the situation and of the   ▶▶

relevant aspect of the Christian story. What connections can be made?

Fourth, consider how you see things differently as the result of doing this exercise. Have you arrived at a new way of knowing where God is in the situation?

Fifth, ponder what it means to live theologically, and what action this might involve.

## Further reading

Aveyard, I (1997), *God Thoughts: a starter course in theological reflection*, Nottingham, St John's Extension Studies.

Ballard, P and Pritchard, J (1996), *Practical Theology in Action*, London, SPCK.

Bevans, S B (1992), *Models of Contextual Theology*, Maryknoll, New York, Orbis.

Browning, D (1991), *A Fundamental Practical Theology*, Minneapolis, Minnesota, Fortress.

Green, L (1990), *Let's Do Theology*, London, Mowbray.

Schreiter, R (1985), *Constructing Local Theologies*, Maryknoll, Orbis.

# 10. WALKING WITH CHRIST

## Introduction

This chapter draws together a number of threads which have been woven throughout the book. The chapter revisits the characters who have revealed something of what it means to live theology and asks you to extend some of their stories and their theologies. Standing back from the particular instances of living theology, the chapter also seeks to integrate the different elements of the theological enterprise within a model of living theology, represented in figure 2. It will be seen that this model involves a multi-dimensional dialogue between the present situation and the Christian tradition, at the heart of which lies the possibility of encounter with the living God.

---

*Reflecting on experience*
Revisit the questions asked at the beginning of chapter 1 in order to see how your answers have changed:

What does theology mean to me?

What is my starting point for exploring living theology?

Where do I begin to do theology?

What important experiences do I bring with me?

## The process of living theology

On the day of the resurrection, according to Luke 24:13–35, two of the disciples were going to a village called Emmaus. While they were talking together, Jesus came near and went with them, though they did not recognise him. They told him of the events of the past few days and expressed something of their sorrow and confusion. Jesus called them foolish and slow for not recognising what was happening before their very eyes and, beginning with Moses and all the prophets, he interpreted to them the things about himself in all the scriptures. When they came near to Emmaus they begged Jesus to stay with them, and at table they recognised him in the breaking of bread.

The story of the road to Emmaus has all the elements of living theology. The context is a journey. The two friends are journeying from the events of the first Easter, unclear in their understanding and unable to see the Christ who comes and walks with them. They do not initially see and know him, although their hearts burn within them as he explains the scriptures and teaches them about himself. The friends are not alone. They travel together and are part of the community of disciples that have followed Jesus thus far. In the dialogue between their present and the tradition of their faith they encounter the risen Christ. Their action was to witness to him.

Their journey is one of a number that have been woven together by St Luke in his narrative of the events of Easter. The high priest, Pilate, Simon of Cyrene, Joseph of Arimathea and the criminals crucified with Jesus all had journeys that led them to the cross of Jesus, to be part of something that they did not understand but helped to unfold. The women had been on a journey to the tomb and had returned with an incredible story told to them by angels, an idle tale according to the men. But Peter, whose personal journey over the past three days had led him to disown Jesus, ran to the tomb and found it empty. Later Christ appeared to him, and then to the disciples gathered together. All found their encounter with Jesus was critical to their own future but was also part of the bigger story of salvation history.

We have encountered a number of individuals as this book has progressed and their stories also fit into a broader picture, in this instance the way to live theology. In chapter 1 we met Jo who experienced a deeply spiritual moment walking in the mountains. We met David who suddenly realised while receiving communion that Jesus was committed to sharing in the world's suffering. Sally the social worker met with her vicar and found a fellow traveller committed to changing the unjust structures of society. Janet came to church seeking a better hope and found that it helped her to live in the present. Michael encountered a silence beyond words in Julian's cell. Alan found a new way of studying the scriptures and Sheila discovered God through her work as a physicist. Each found that a moment of encounter was to change the direction of their lives and stimulate them to walk with Christ by beginning to live theology.

In chapter 2 we met Judith, Sandra, Andrew, Diane and Graham. All had recognised the way that their past experience was affecting the way that they lived their lives and understood their faith in the present. Chapter 3 introduced us to Janet, Bill and Brian. These three had begun to explore the history and contexts in which their church communities lived and worked. They had recognised the need to explore and examine these situations as an important part of the process of doing theology.

Chapter 4 introduced us to Michael, who was serving eighteen months in a young offender's institution, and John who was struggling to understand him. He was wondering whether to visit Michael and for what purpose. Making up a 'thick description' of the situation helped him to develop a broader understanding of what was happening but left him unsure how he could relate this to the scripture and tradition of the faith. How John and Michael's story could be in dialogue or conversation with the stories of the faith community was not resolved at this point.

Chapter 8 introduced us to Sue. A trip to the shop to buy her son a pair of trainers introduced her to the way in which our thinking and actions are governed by ideas and attitudes that come from pre-modern, modern and post-modern understandings of the world. Sue was left with a difficult choice although she had helped us to a better understanding of society today.

In chapter 9 we encountered Tom. His problem stemmed from a difficult situation at work but, with the help of a group of Christians from the local church, he was able to work through that situation and come to a view on what he should do. The richly textured story that he was able to construct about his present situation encountered similarly richly textured stories that he and the group were able to construct from the scriptures and tradition of the church. This led to a dialogue between the two that, in the power of the Holy Spirit, produced a way forward for him.

The disciples on the road to Emmaus *journeyed with Jesus* from the tomb into the future so that their encounter was part of an on-going faith experience. They were part of the *community of faith* whose members experienced Christ together and supported and helped one another. They shared the *context* provided by their history and present situation. They sought to *see and know Christ* in the situation. They engaged in a *dialogue with the scripture and tradition*. They *acted* by witnessing to the risen Christ. The *story* that they were able to tell about themselves, their tradition and their encounter with the risen Christ gave meaning to their witness, and Luke's story has given us access to his interpretation of that encounter which, in turn, can inform our present.

In the individual stories, and in particular in the stories of Tom and of the disciples on the road to Emmaus, we encounter a living theology which can be expressed in the following way.

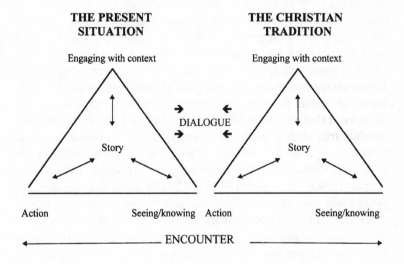

Figure 2

Like any diagram, this way of understanding living theology has its advantages and its limitations. It shows clearly that at the heart of living theology is the conversation or dialogue that takes place between the present situation and the scripture and tradition of our church in the power of the Holy Spirit. It is of course a conversation that happens in a series of important dimensions.

One such dimension is provided by the faith community. First, the journey is undertaken with others and our work of living theology is infinitely richer for the way that the community can help and support the individual in this process. Second, the community has been formed around key foundational texts that emerged during the first four centuries. Therefore, both the church's credal statements and the canon of scripture provide necessary boundaries and important arenas in which theology is practised. Third, the church itself lives and works 'between the times', an agent of the Kingdom, experiencing God imperfectly in the present but looking for ultimate fulfilment in the future.

Another important dimension is provided by the history that individuals and groups bring to this process. To be self-aware is a critical starting point for living theology. To be able to identify and evaluate the beliefs, attitudes, values and agendas that have emerged from our past to inform our present is to know the biases that we bring to any problem. To know the history that has formed a group is to know the pre-understandings that it will bring to any new situation. And of course the culture in which we live provides a way of seeing and knowing the world that will deeply affect the theological process.

The diagram on page 99 recognises that the process of living theology involves the present situation in which our lives are lived and the tradition that comes down to us. Sometimes it is an incident or crisis in our present that stimulates the need to engage with theology. That was certainly true of Tom in the last chapter. However, when we encountered Alan in chapter 1, we became aware that it was his study of the scriptures that had stimulated him to begin. It is possible to begin with the present or with the tradition, but whichever is the starting point, the process will inevitably lead to a dialogue between these contexts in order to stimulate an appropriate outcome or action. Also, the process can be begun at any point represented on the triangle. It could be an action that requires investigation, a context that needs to be examined or an insight that needs to be explored. Any of these could be the starting point for developing a thick description and investigating the story or stories that could be told from a variety of perspectives. A thick description of any of these will highlight the rich story that is being told and establish creative points of contact between the tradition and the present context.

Tom and his friends also learned that to live theology effectively is to learn humility, to be open to God and to the contribution of other people, to be able to see through the eyes of others, to be changed and to change, and to be prepared to act in line with the demands of God's Kingdom.

To live theology is to encounter God. The word 'encounter' appears in the diagram, but is not specific to any part of the process. Living theology is always practised in openness to the work of the Holy Spirit, and this model provides the possibility for significant encounters with other people and with God at many points in the process. Insight and transformation may therefore occur at any moment and this will lead to new ways of understanding the situation and give new possibilities for action.

---

**EXERCISE**

Revisit Brian and Bill in chapter 3. Brian had been attempting to make a thick description of the area in which his church was set. He already knew that genuine poverty existed, that a lack of public transport was restricting the ability of some members of the community to visit friends or shops, that some young mothers were without necessary support and that some elderly people were lonely. He also recognised that an appropriate response to this might involve the church in undertaking some remedial work themselves while working for political change. He had therefore begun to develop a thick description of the present situation.

Do some further work on Brian's thick description. Write on postcards the key details of the different stories and perspectives that were emerging. Use your imagination. Develop further perspectives. Use your knowledge of the community in which you live. Use the questions outlined in chapter 4. (Be particularly aware of any groups or individuals who may be disadvantaged and other groups or individuals who are unduly advantaged.)

Engage with scripture and tradition. What is your first point of contact? (Is it for example the texts in Luke which relate to the poor, that were encountered in Tom's story?) Then, how might you see the bigger story? Again, the objective is to move from thin to thick description. Record different perspectives on postcards once more.    ▶▶

Explore the dialogue between the two thick descriptions, those of the situation and of the relevant aspect of the Christian story (using the postcards to help you). What connections can be made?

Consider how you see things differently as the result of doing this exercise. Have you arrived at a new way of knowing where God is in the situation?

Ponder what it would mean for Brian's church to live theologically, and what action this might involve.

**EXERCISE**

Revisit Sue in chapter 8. Sue had begun to build up a thick description of the incident in the shop where she and other parents had been buying trainers for their children. She had noted the different reactions of the parents and had begun to build up a picture of what was happening.

Using your imagination, develop the thick description of the situation. Use the questions outlined in chapter 4. (Consider for example the role of the shoe shop and the way trainers are advertised. Explore the contexts in which the youngsters will wear their trainers, etc.)

Engage with scripture and tradition. What is your first point of contact? (Might it be texts which suggest that a recognition of the Kingdom of God involves not being over-concerned with material things, for example Matthew 6:25–34?) Then, how might you see the bigger story? Again, the objective is to move from thin to thick description. Record different perspectives on postcards once more.

Explore the dialogue between the two thick descriptions, those of the situation and of the relevant aspect of the Christian story (using the postcards to help you). What connections can be made? ▶▶

Consider how you see things differently as the result of doing this exercise. Have you arrived at a new way of knowing where God is in the situation?

Ponder what it would mean for Sue to live theologically at that time, and what action this might involve. Remember that there are no 'right' or 'wrong' answers.

## Where do I go from here?

It is possible that you may have read this book in order to prepare for a course of study. If that is so then you might need to consider what support you will need to be able to undertake that work in the future. If you are not preparing for a particular course then you might consider looking around to see what opportunities for theological study there are in your area. Colleges of further and higher education may well be worth investigating and the church will often provide opportunities for further study through the local or broader church; for example, most Church of England dioceses run some courses. You will also find a good selection of distance learning courses available.

Some of the courses provided by colleges, local churches and dioceses give opportunities for general theological education, while some prepare individuals for specific areas of ministry. It is therefore worth taking time and care in considering what is appropriate for you. This book is one of a series that will build towards the Church Colleges' Certificate, and this may be an appropriate way forward.

If you join a course through church or college then you may be asked to work in a variety of different ways: with a supervisor, in seminar or study groups. If you do not join such a course (or even if you do) it might be worth setting up an informal group with friends or with other members of your local church congregation. You might already belong to a study or prayer group or meet to study with a group of people during Lent. You can see from Tom's experience that such a group can come alive when it is challenged to deal with real situations and is asked to make thick, rather than thin, descriptions of the situation under investigation and of scripture and tradition. To work in community is to be supported and challenged by other people as we work to bring fruitful action out of the encounter between the present and the scripture and tradition of the church. The gifts of the Spirit that are shared out among members of a church group will bring a richness to the work of theology and will place it where it is often most creative, in the hearts and minds and lives and work of ordinary Christians who are gathered in Christ's name. To live theology is to be in a community that prays and studies and, although it is possible and sometimes necessary for Christians to think things through alone, there is no substitute for the support and insight of other people.

Tom and his group worked with integrity. They read as widely as they could and used the fruits of scholarship. It is always necessary to use the skills and knowledge of those who work as full-time theologians and scholars. Their ministry is to explore the faith in their chosen area of expertise and to relate it afresh to each generation. They are guides on the journey and should be consulted through book and commentary at every opportunity.

This course has provided you with a basic reading list. Some of these books will provide further insight into the process of doing theology and some are provided to support your study of the Old Testament, New Testament and the early church. They will help you to decide where your interest for further learning might lie.

Living theology is not easy although it is rewarding. There are often no 'right' answers and no easy shortcuts to seeing and knowing Christ in what are often complex and difficult situations. But there has never been a better time for members of church congregations to equip themselves through living theology to be effective witnesses of the Gospel and workers for Christ in every area of life.

---

**EXERCISE**

Address the following questions:

- What areas of theological study would I like to develop?
- Who shall I do theology with?

Identify the resources that you will need.

# Further reading

Craig, Y (1994), *Learning for Life*, London, Mowbray.

Donovan, V (1982), *Christianity Rediscovered*, London, SCM.

General Synod Board of Education (1996), *Tomorrow is Another Country: postmodernism and Christian education*, London, Church House Publishing.

Holloway, R (1997), *Dancing on the Edge*, London, HarperCollins.

# REFERENCES

à Kempis, T (1962), *The Imitation of Christ*, London, Fontana.

Barrett, C K (1957), *A Commentary on the Epistle to the Romans*, London, A and C Black, Eerdmans.

Bauckham, R (ed.) (1998), *The Gospels for All Christians*, Grand Rapids, Michigan, Eerdmans.

Bigger, S (ed.) (1989), *Creating the Old Testament*, Oxford, Blackwell.

Bradshaw, P (1996), *Early Christian Worship*, London, SPCK.

Browning, D (1991), *A Fundamental Practical Theology*, Minneapolis, Minnesota, Fortress.

Bruner, J (1990), *Acts of Meaning*, Cambridge, Massachusetts, Harvard University Press.

Burridge, R (1992), *What are the Gospels?*, Cambridge, Cambridge University Press.

Clines, D (1978), *The Theme of the Pentateuch*, Sheffield, JSOT Press.

Court, J M (1997), *Reading the New Testament*, London, Routledge.

Denzin, N (1987), *Interpretive Biography*, Newbury Park, California, Sage.

Fiorenza, E S (1983), *In Memory of Her*, London, SCM.

General Synod Board of Education, *Tomorrow is Another Country: post-modernism and Christian education*, London, Church House Publishing.

Giddens, A (1990), *The Consequences of Modernity*, Cambridge, Polity Press.

Knapp, P (1990), *Chaucer and the Social Conquest*, New York, Routledge.

Limburg, J (1992), *Jonah*, London, SCM.

Macquarrie, J (1966), *Principles of Christian Theology*, London, SCM.

Moltmann, J (1974), *The Crucified God*, London, SCM.

Mother Teresa (1986), *Meditations on the Way of the Cross*, London, Mowbray.

Rowland, C (1988), *Radical Christianity*, Cambridge, Polity Press.

Theissen, G (1982), *The Social Setting of Pauline Christianity*, Edinburgh, T and T Clark.

Tillich, P (1978), *Systematic Theology* (volume 3), London, SCM.

Young, F (1991), *The Making of the Creeds*, London, SCM.

# Applying for the Church Colleges' Certificate Programme

The certificate programme is available in Anglican Church Colleges of Higher Education throughout England and Wales. There are currently hundreds of students on this programme, many with no previous experience of study of this kind. There are no entry requirements. Some people choose to take Certificate courses for their own interest and personal growth, others take these courses as part of their training for ministry in the church. Some go on to complete the optional assignments and, after the successful completion of three courses, gain the Certificate. Courses available through the *Exploring Faith: theology for life* series are ideal for establishing ability and potential for studying theology and biblical studies at degree level, and they provide credit onto degree programmes.

For further details of the Church Colleges' Certificate programme, related to this series, please contact the person responsible for Adult Education in your local diocese or one of the colleges at the addresses provided:

The Administrator of Part-time Programmes, Department of Theology and Religious Studies, Chester College, Parkgate Road, CHESTER, CH1 4BJ ☎ 01244 375444

The Registry, Roehampton Institute, Froebel College, Roehampton Lane, LONDON, SW15 5PJ ☎ 0181 392 3087

The Registry, Canterbury Christ Church University College, North Holmes Road, CANTERBURY, CT1 1QU ☎ 01227 767700

The Registry, College of St Mark and St John, Derriford Road, PLYMOUTH, PL6 8BH ☎ 01752 636892

The Registry, Trinity College, CARMARTHEN, Carmarthenshire, SA31 3EP ☎ 01267 676804 (direct)

Church Colleges' Programme, The Registry, King Alfred's College, Sparkford Road, WINCHESTER, SO22 4NR ☎ 01962 841515

Part-time Programmes, The Registry, College of St Martin, Bowerham Road, LANCASTER, LA1 3JD ☎ 01524 384529